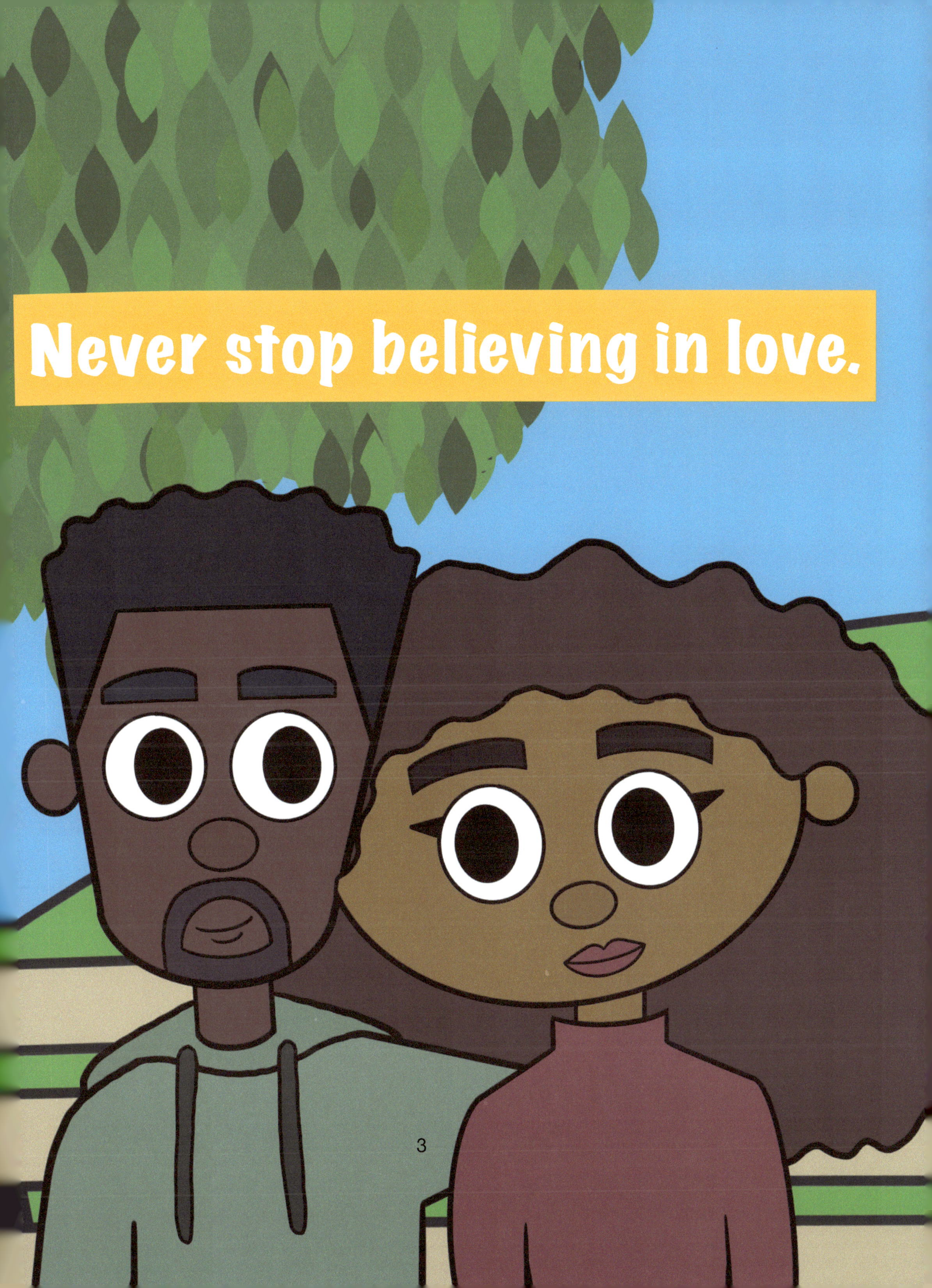

Never stop believing in love.

Published in Los Angeles, California

Website: www.truelovestorybook.com

To contact author: truelovestorybook@gmail.com

Illustration by Bri Bolden

Table of Contents

<u>Based on a True Love Story</u> is loosely based on real experiences. This is a story about love and hope. A young man's wish (Devon) to find his dream-girl, a simple wish, from a young man's point of view. With the helpful advice from his sister Andrea, Devon changes his negative view on love and begins to open himself up to it.

Devon's had a hard time both finding and believing in love, until one day....he meets his dream-girl. Could it be the girl that's literally been in his dreams? Does it end well?

Intended for both young readers at home and schools nationwide, this book is meant to inspire kids and young adults to believe that true love still exists. All ages 5+.

Poetry by: <u>Torée Alexandre</u>

Special Thank You to <u>Torée</u>, the poet who helped make this story into a poem.

About Author:

Andre Ozim is an actor, writer and youth mentor born in Oklahoma City, OK to a Nigerian Mother of the Igbo tribe. Andre began writing this book during the 2020 pandemic as he was inspired by friends and family to journal his own past romances, fears, and life events which helped him create a story that young adults of all ages can relate to.

After a loving kiss on the head, Devon's mom tucks him into bed.

He drifts off to sleep, into dreamland he goes, and this same wish of his heart shows.

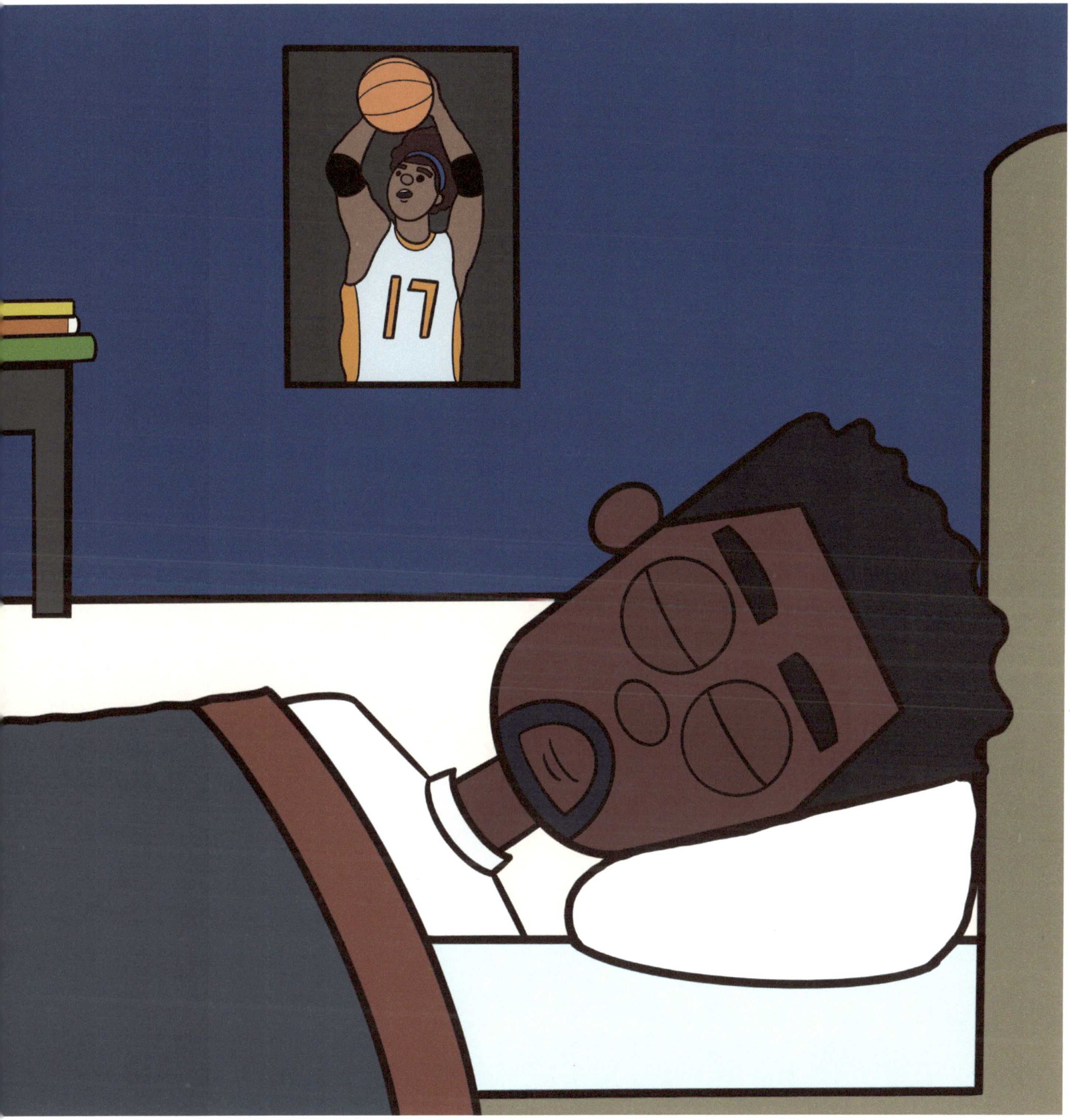
17

In this dream he meets the love of his life,

he proposes to her and she becomes his wife.

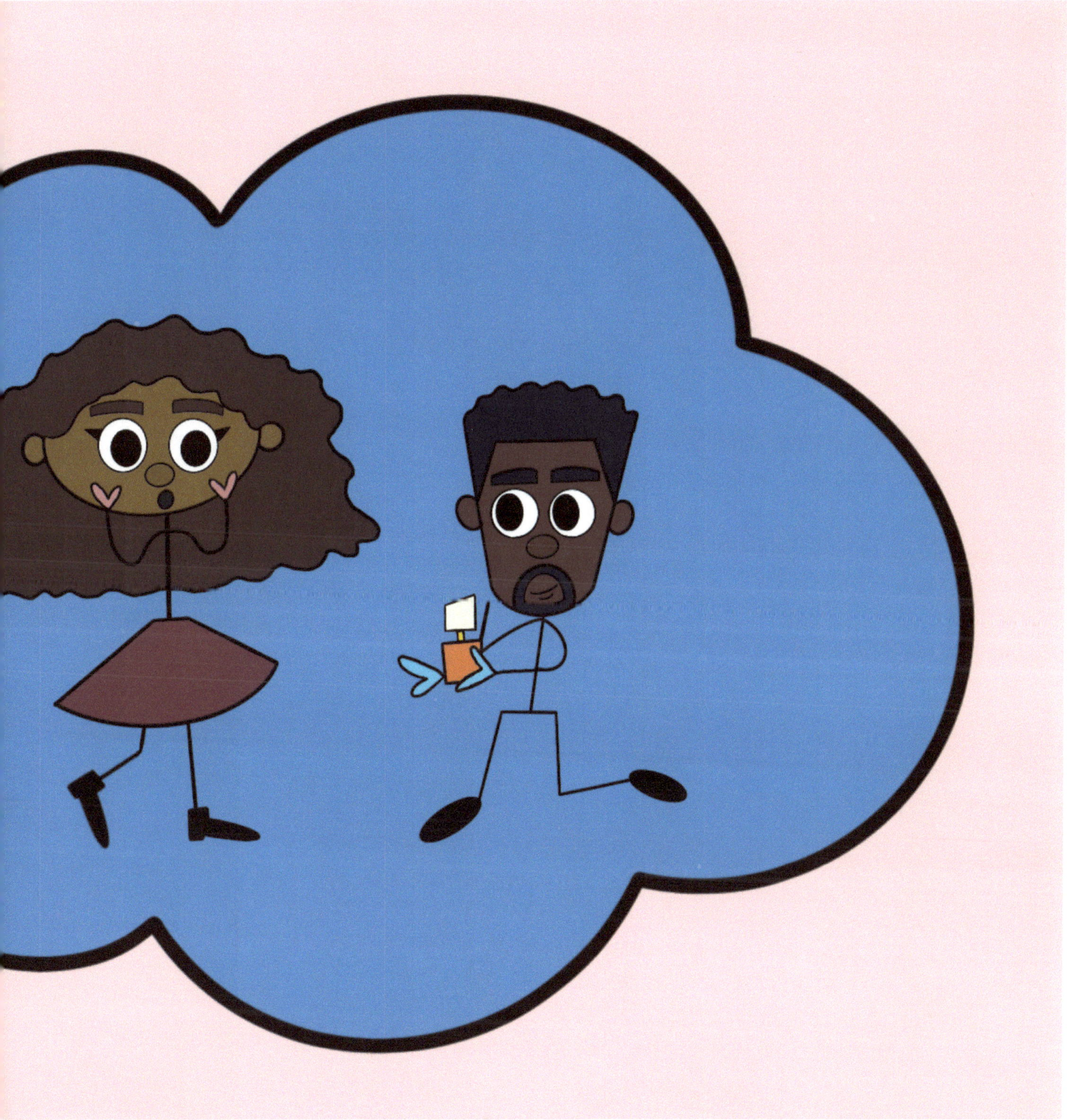

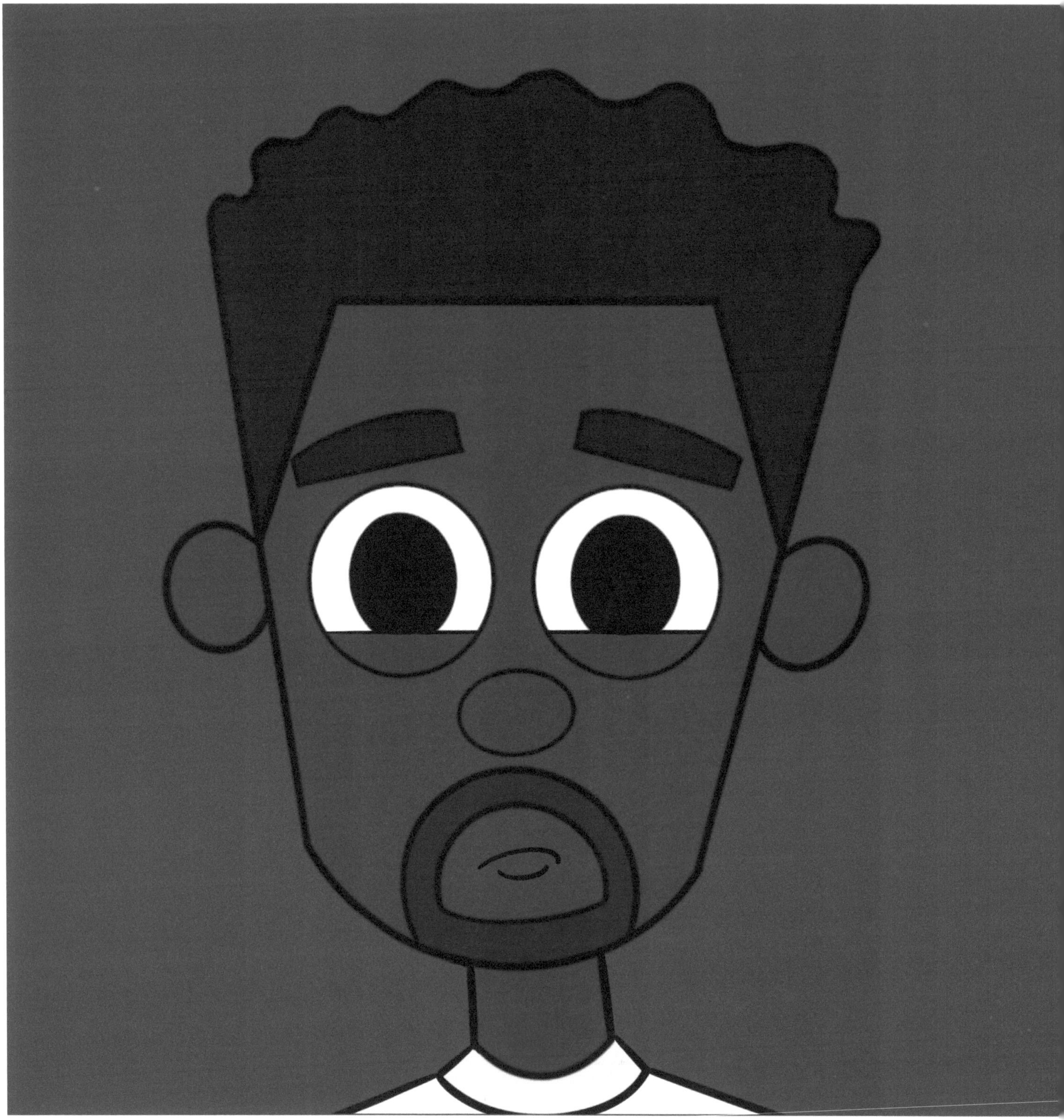

But morning after morning, Devon wakes up alone.

All he really wants is a love of his own.

Believing in love feels like believing in a fairy tale.

Growing up, Devon only saw love around him that would always fail.

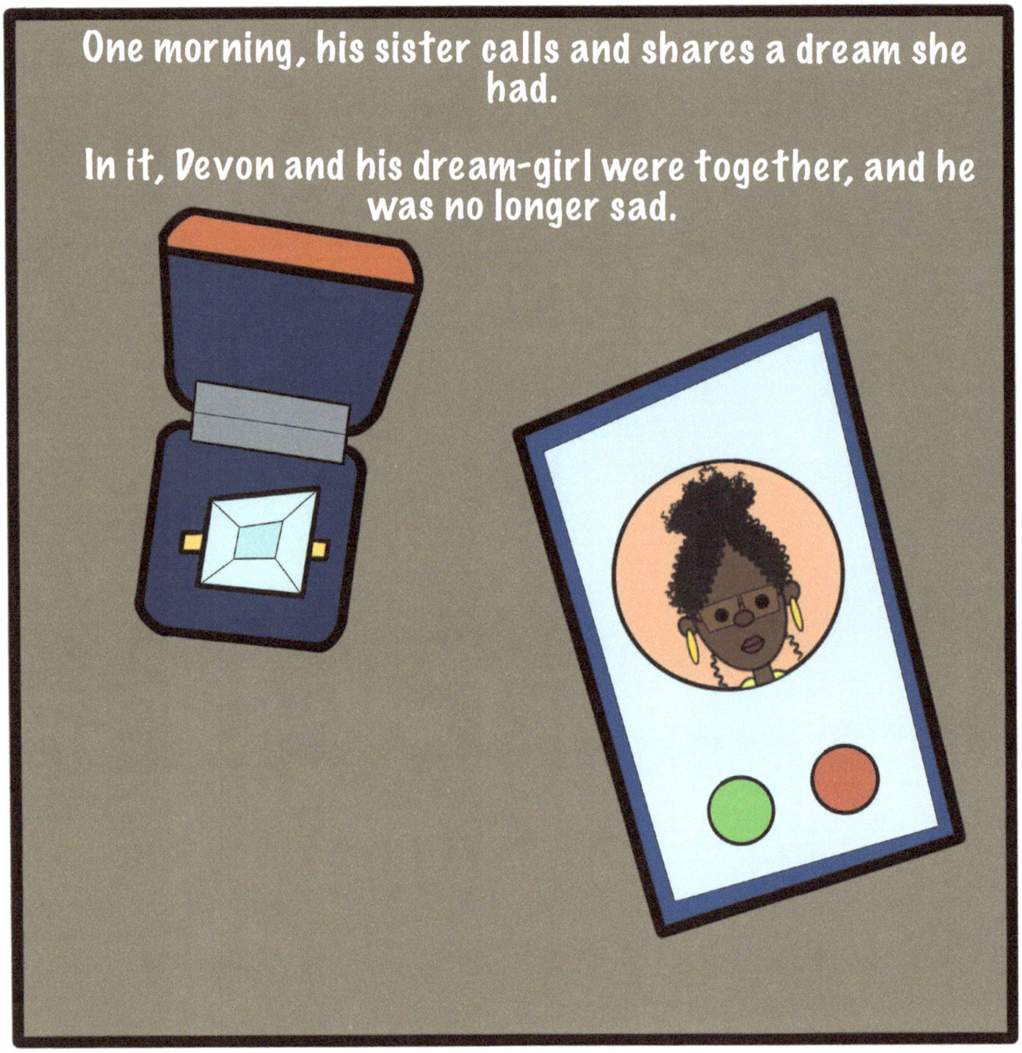
One morning, his sister calls and shares a dream she had.
In it, Devon and his dream-girl were together, and he was no longer sad.

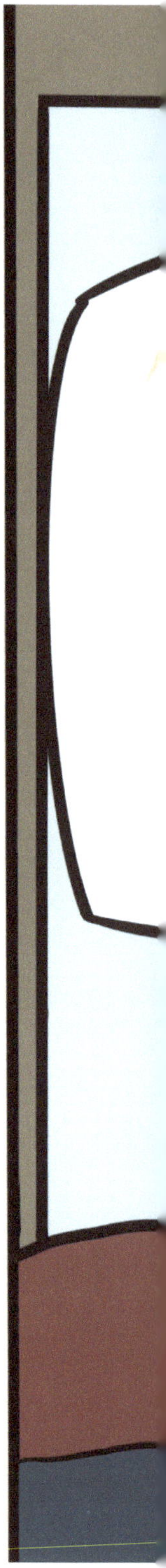

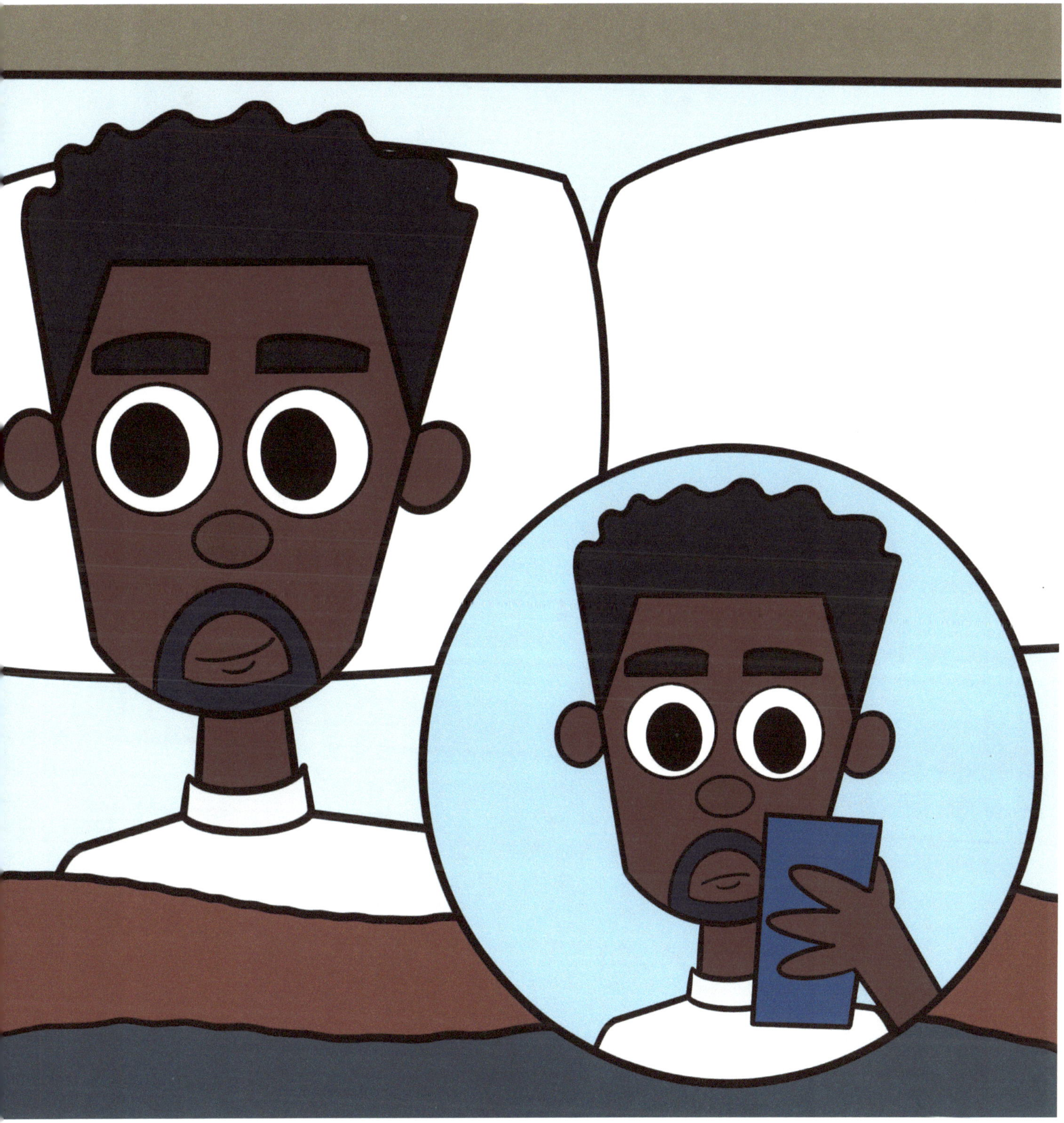

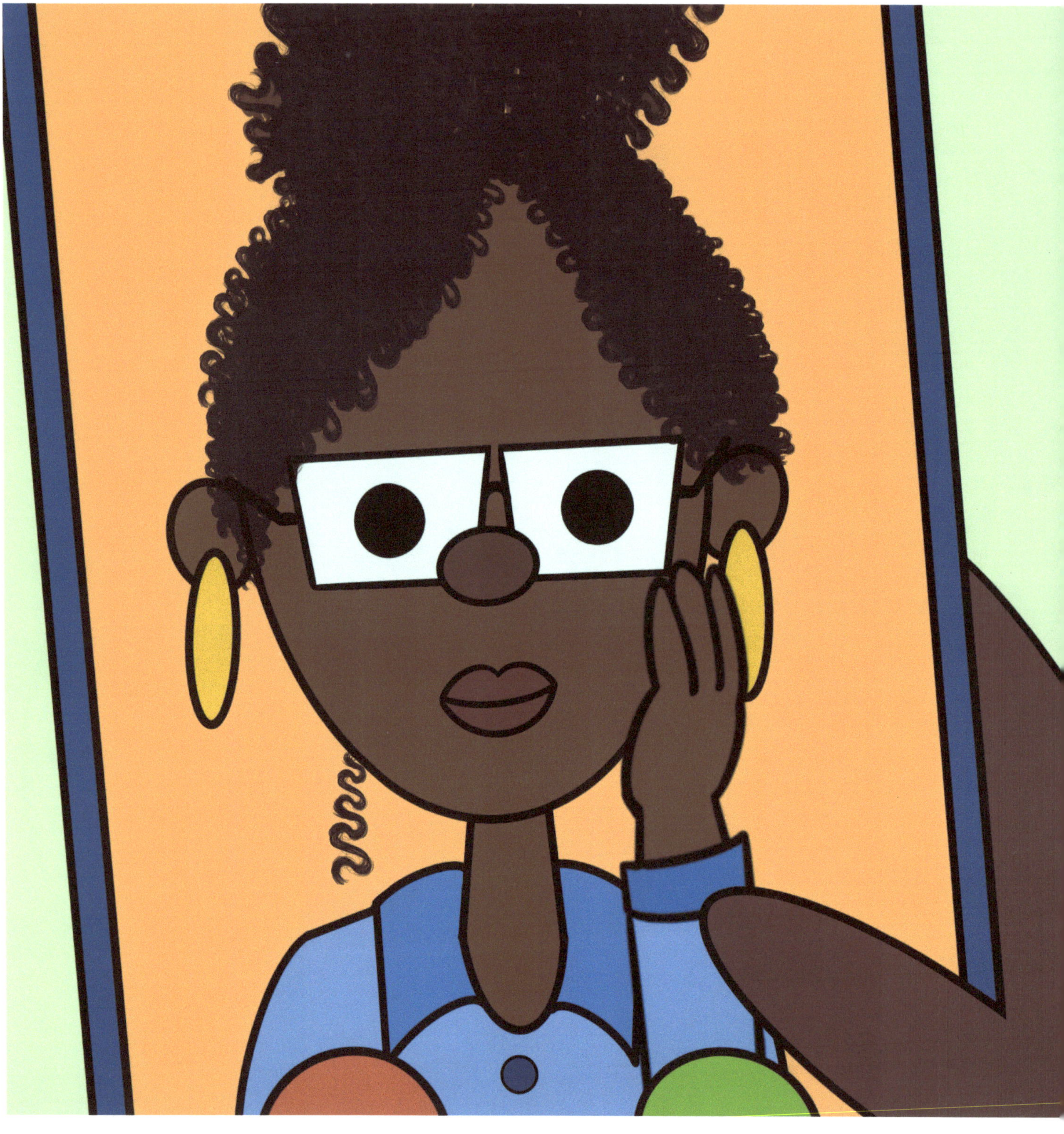

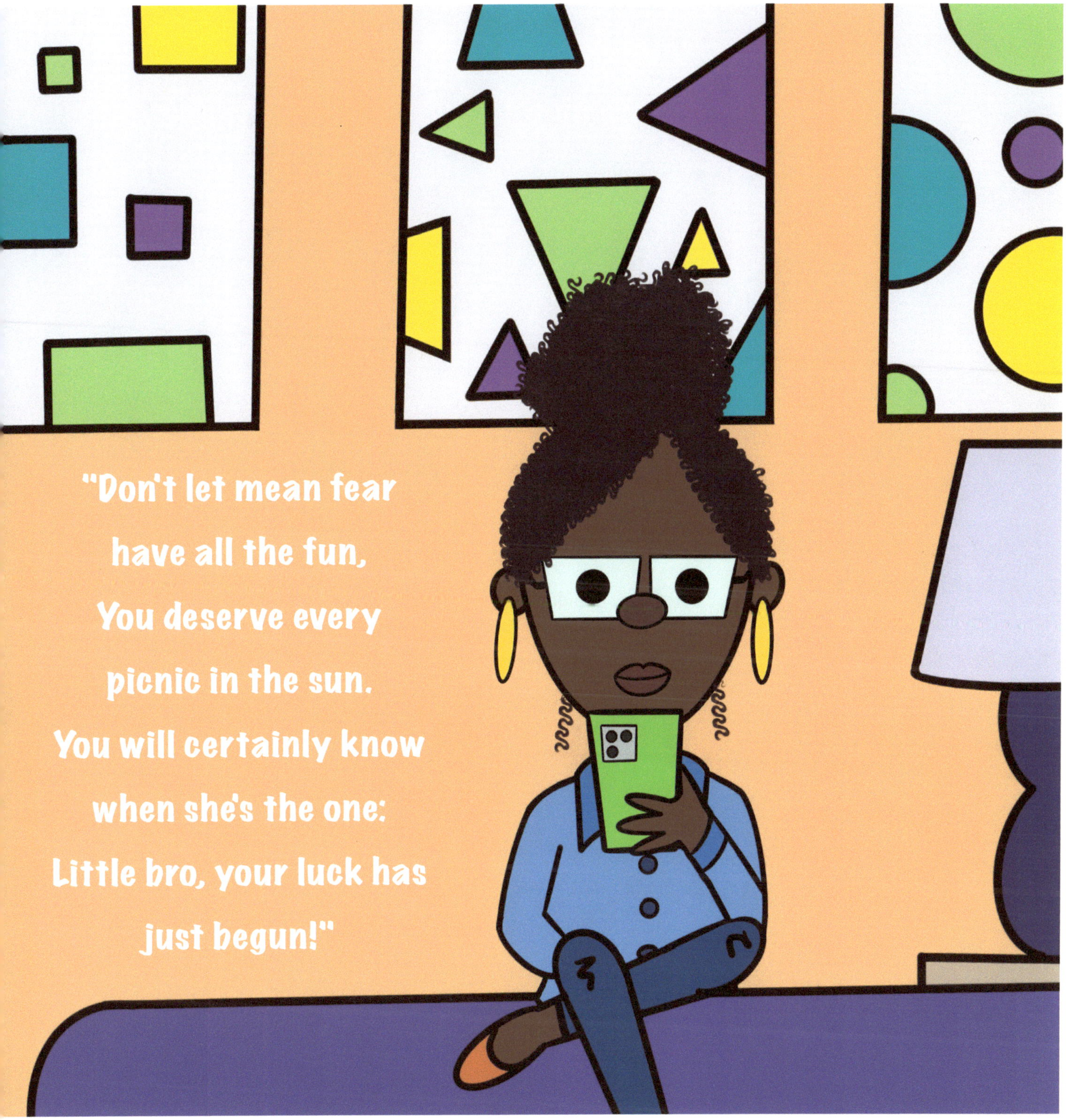

"Don't let mean fear
have all the fun,
You deserve every
picnic in the sun.
You will certainly know
when she's the one:
Little bro, your luck has
just begun!"

Devon feels new hope with the advice

from his sister!

He begins to believe he deserves the woman of his dreams,

and that he will soon be with her!

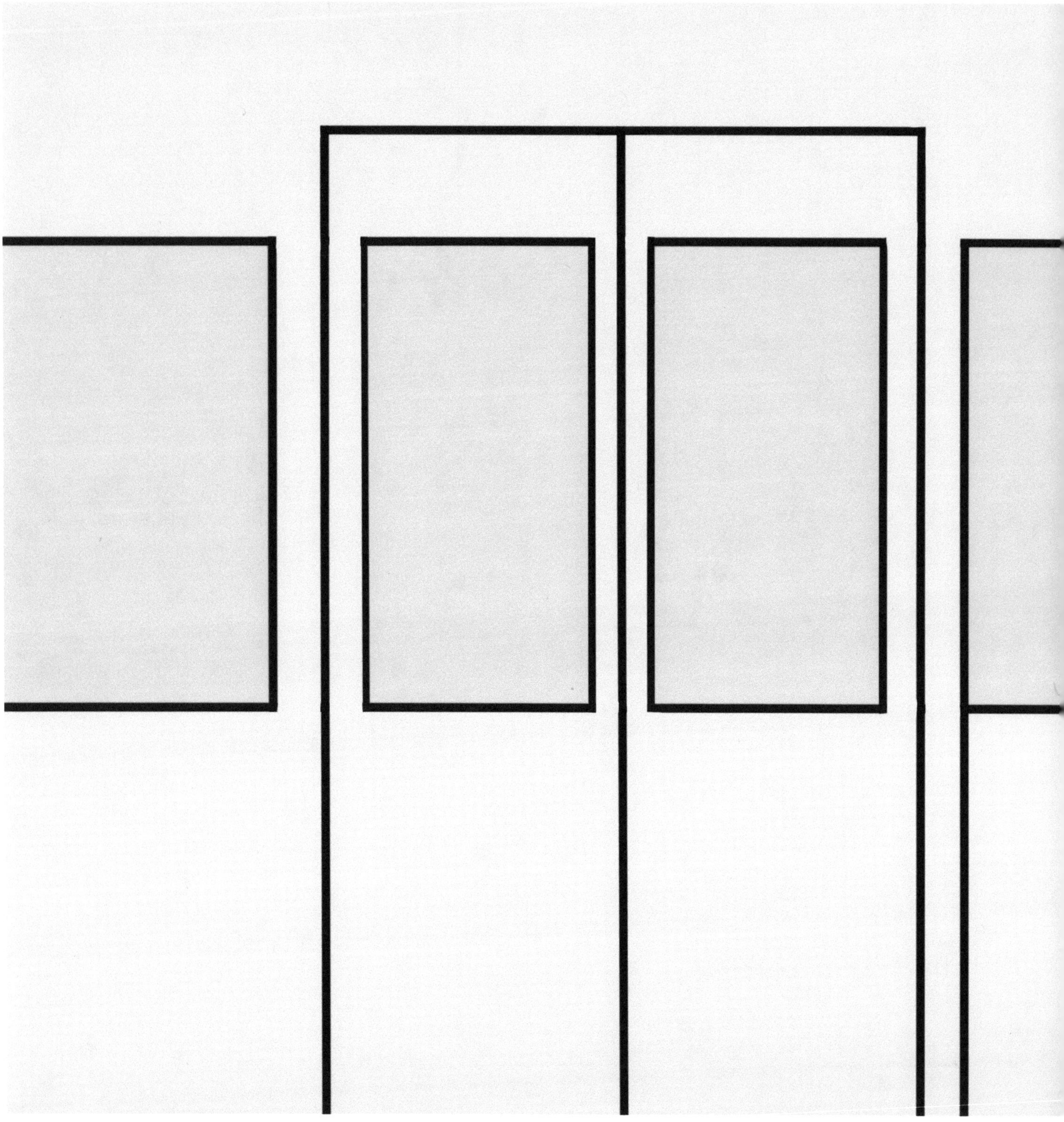

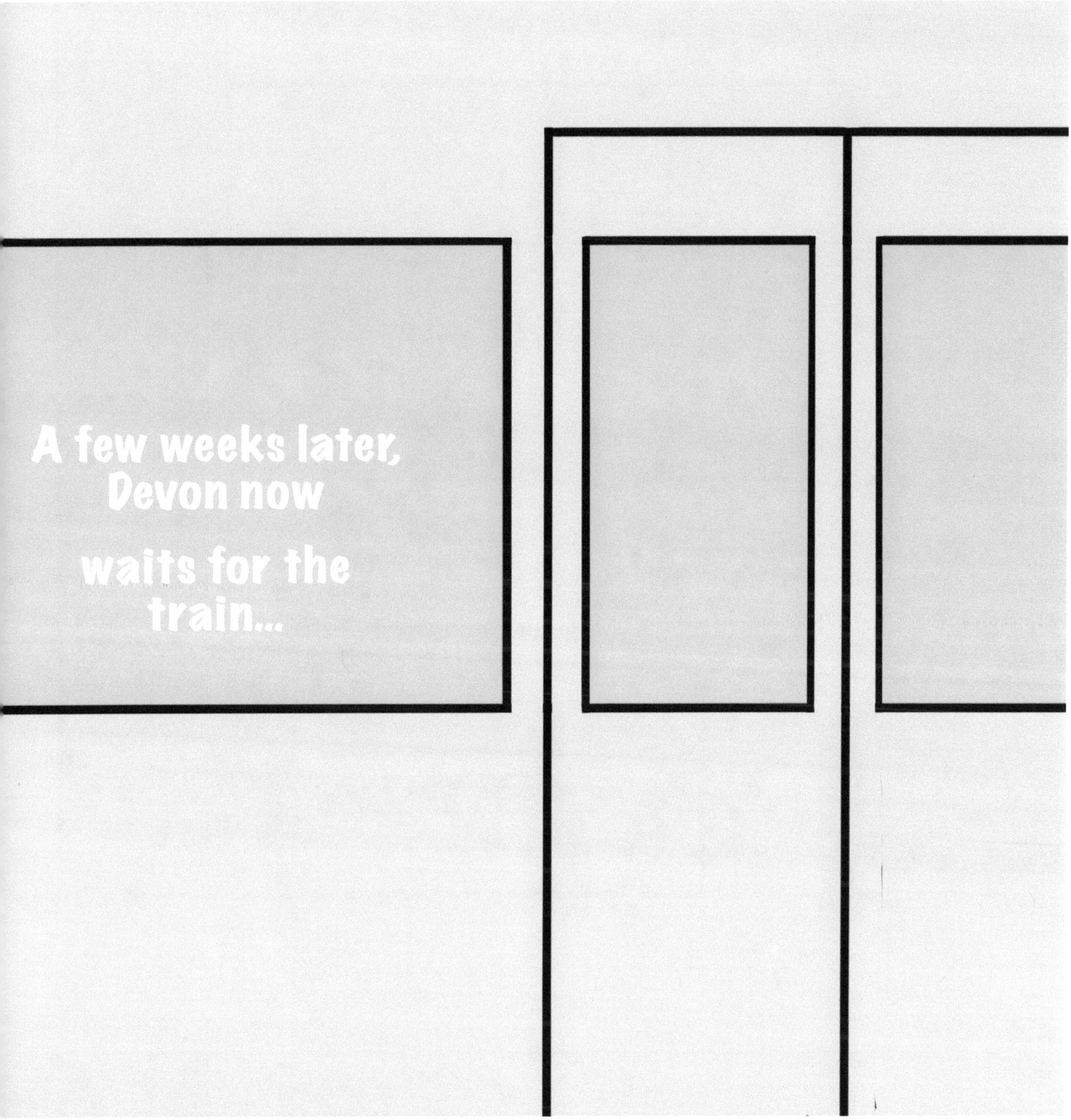
A few weeks later, Devon now waits for the train...

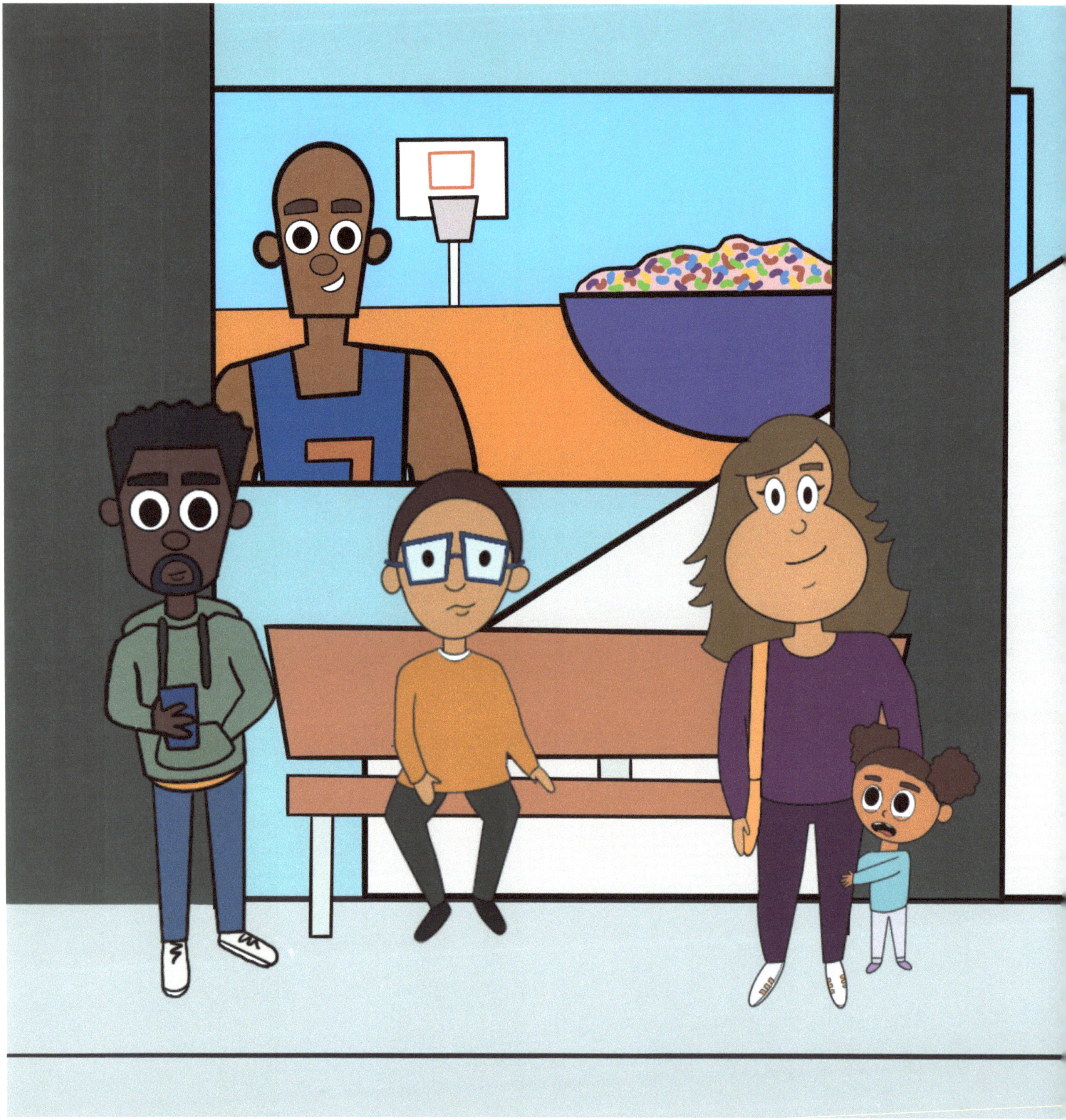

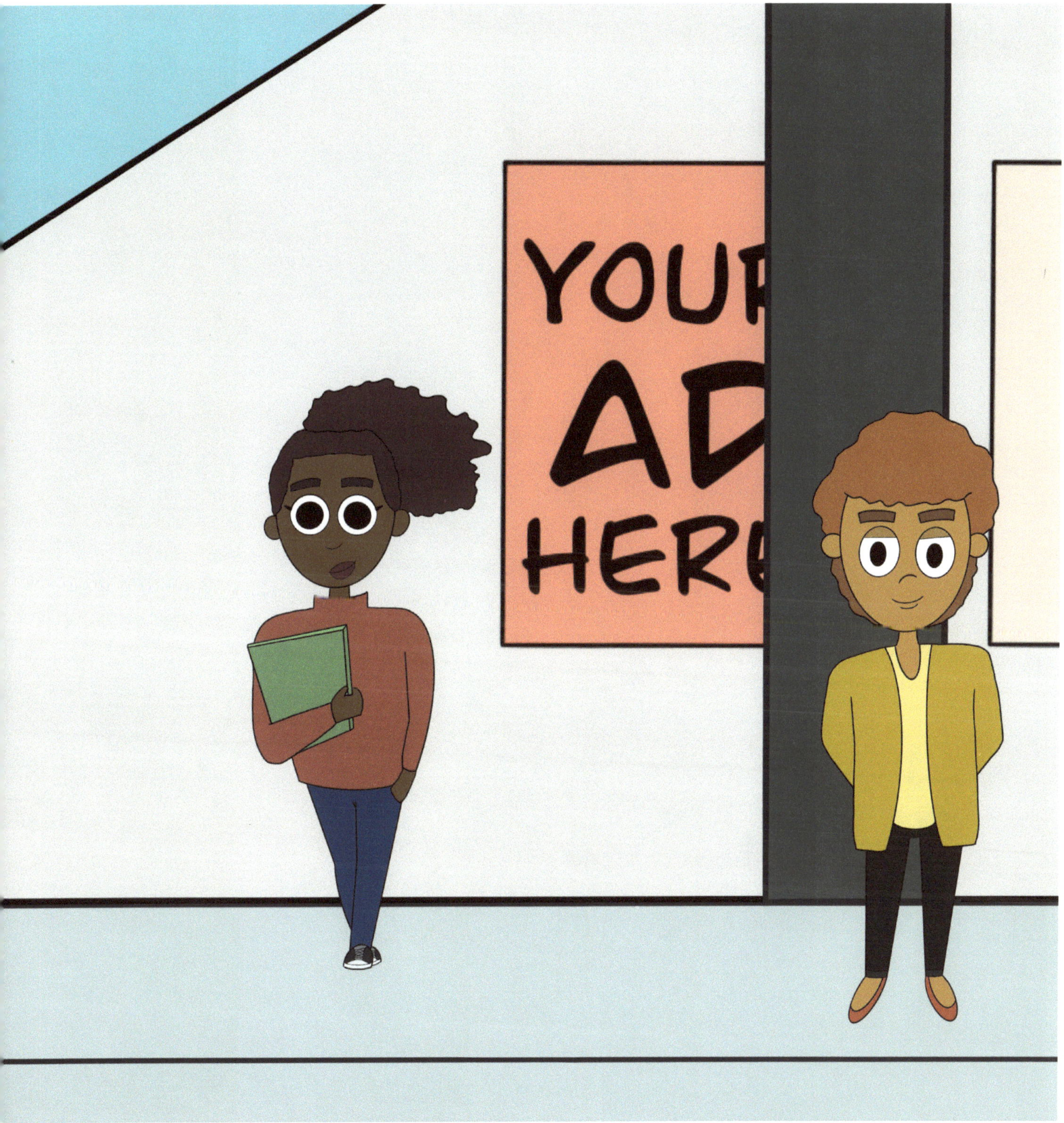
YOUR
AD
HER

Another lovely day heading
into the city,

Devon is on his way...

Then suddenly, he's blinded
by the most

✨ dazzling ray ✨

"Who could that be?!" he
jumps up to say.

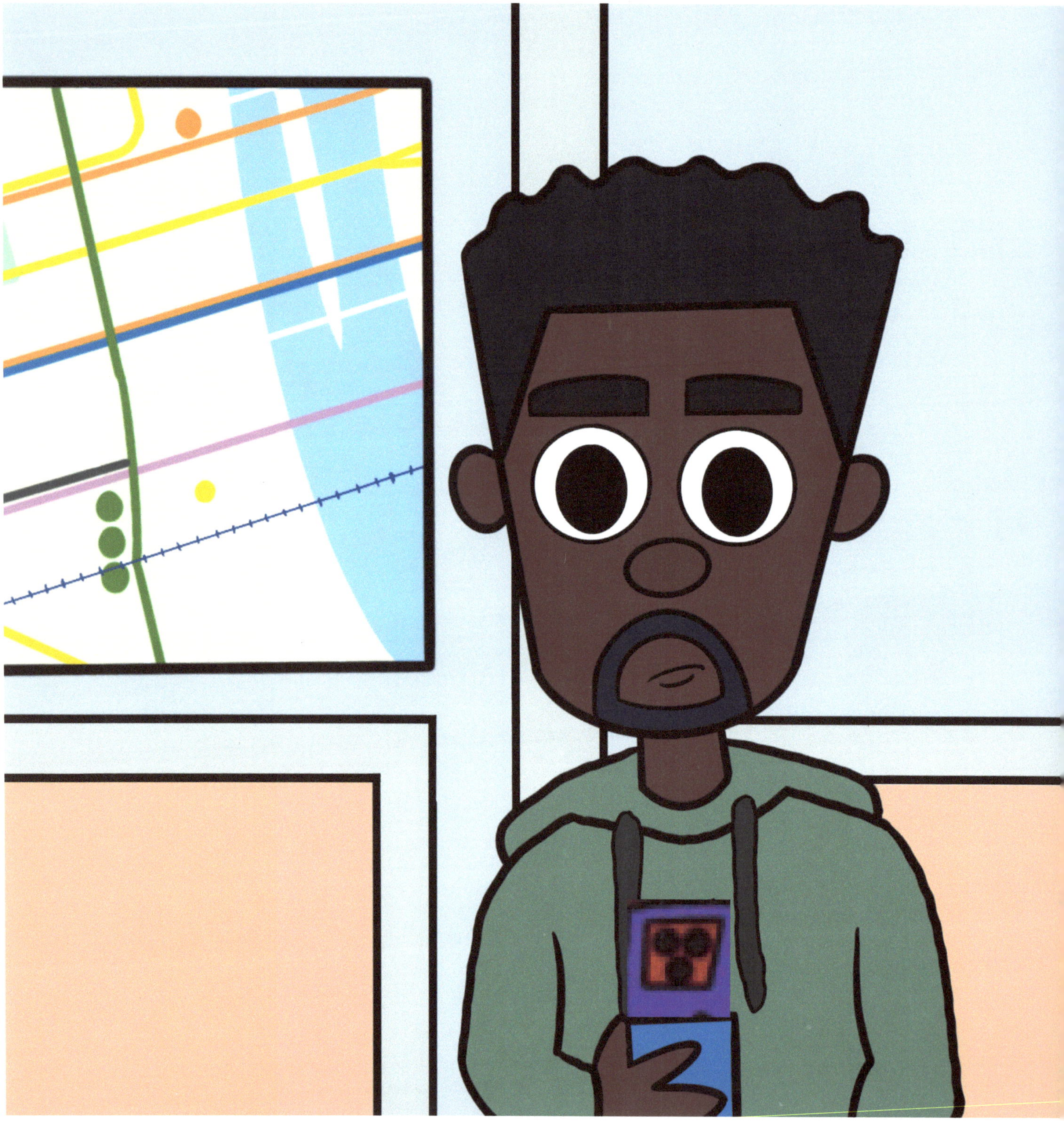

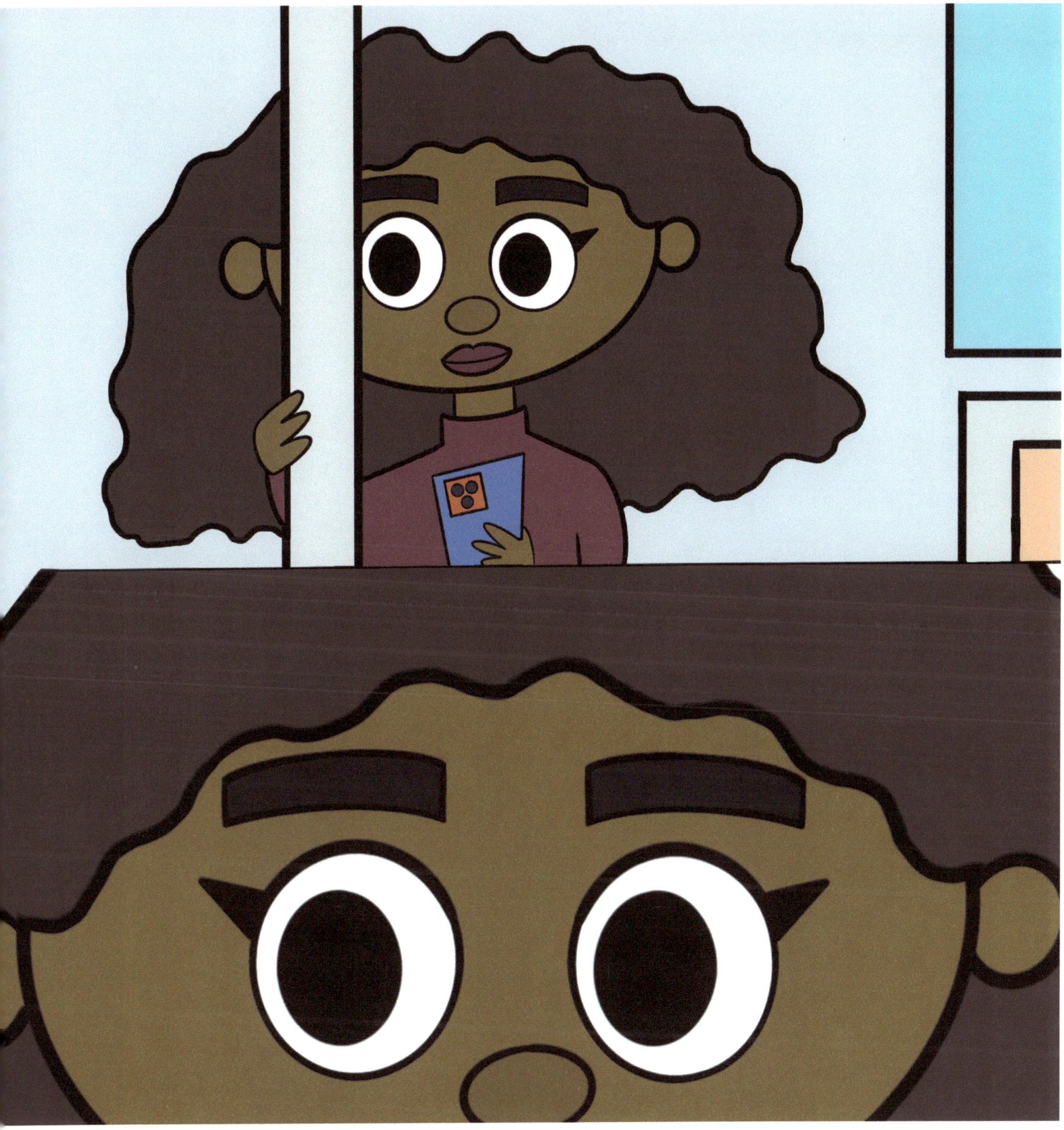

A bright sunshine smile
shines on him from

across the train,

Is it the most beautiful girl
or is Devon going insane...

He pinches himself and tries
to stay zen,

Could this just be Devon
dreaming again?!

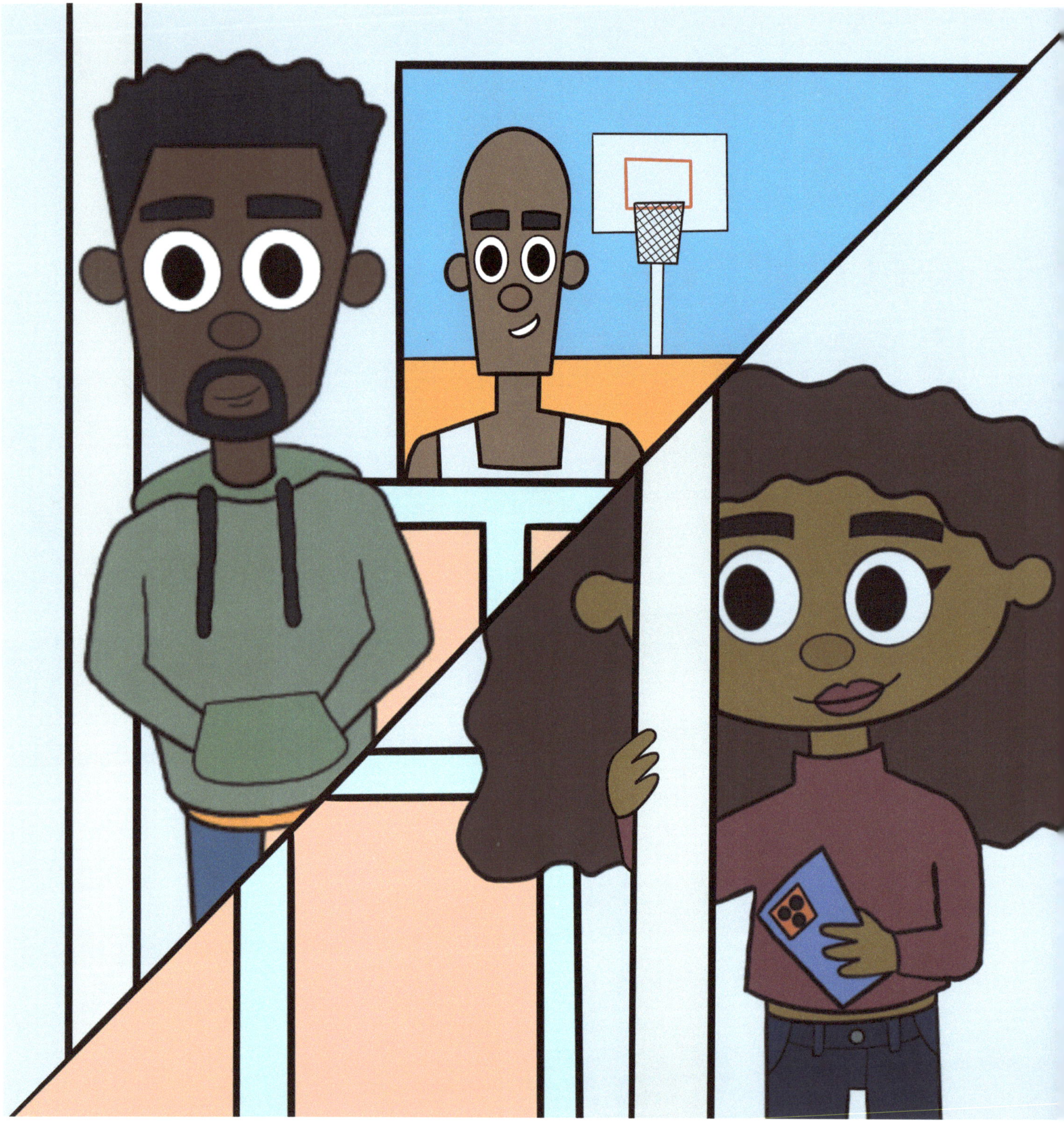

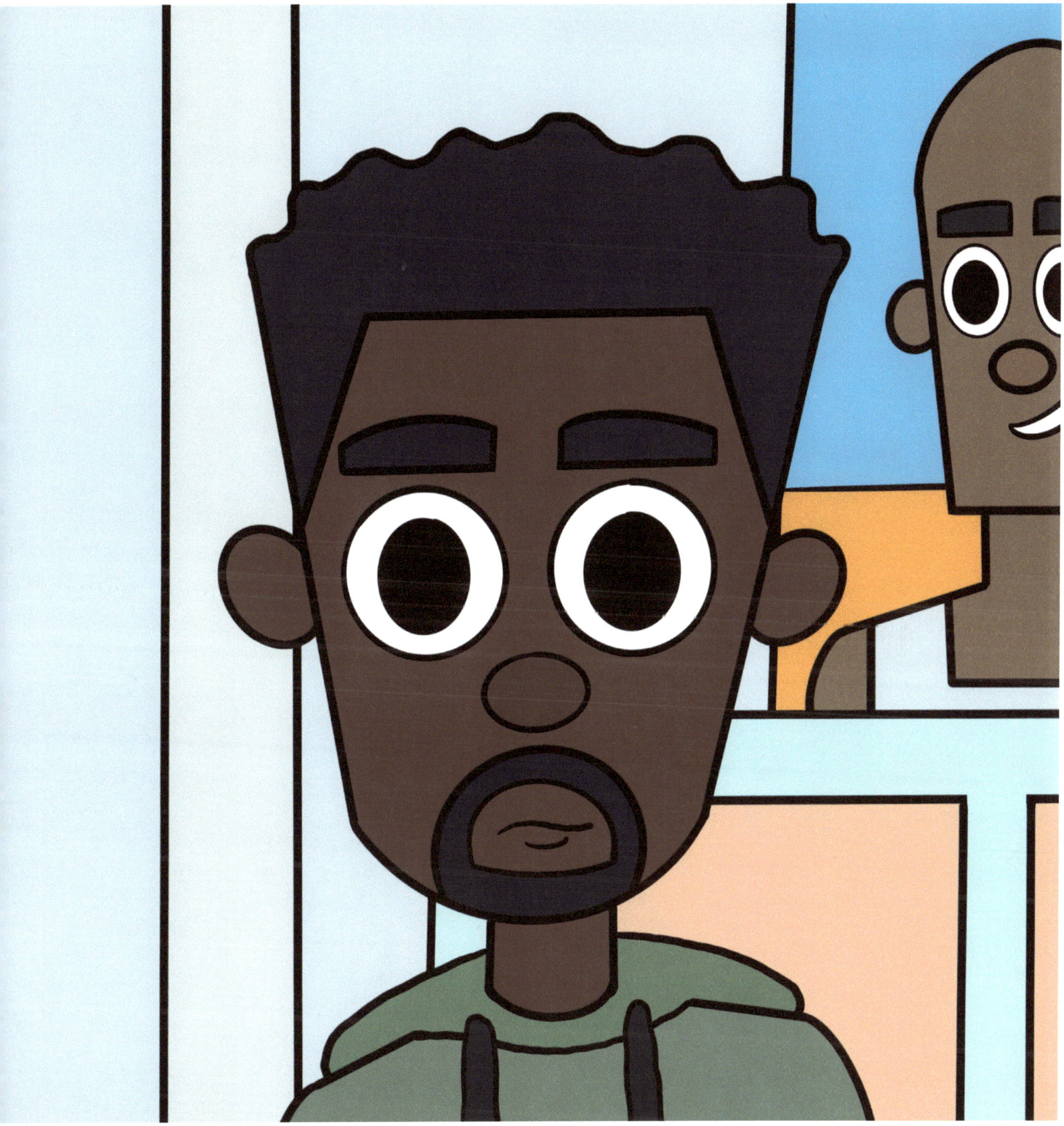

Is this his Dream Girl?

Could this be her?

He blinks one time, two times,
three times, four!

He looks down to see his hands
shaking, then

back up at her once more..

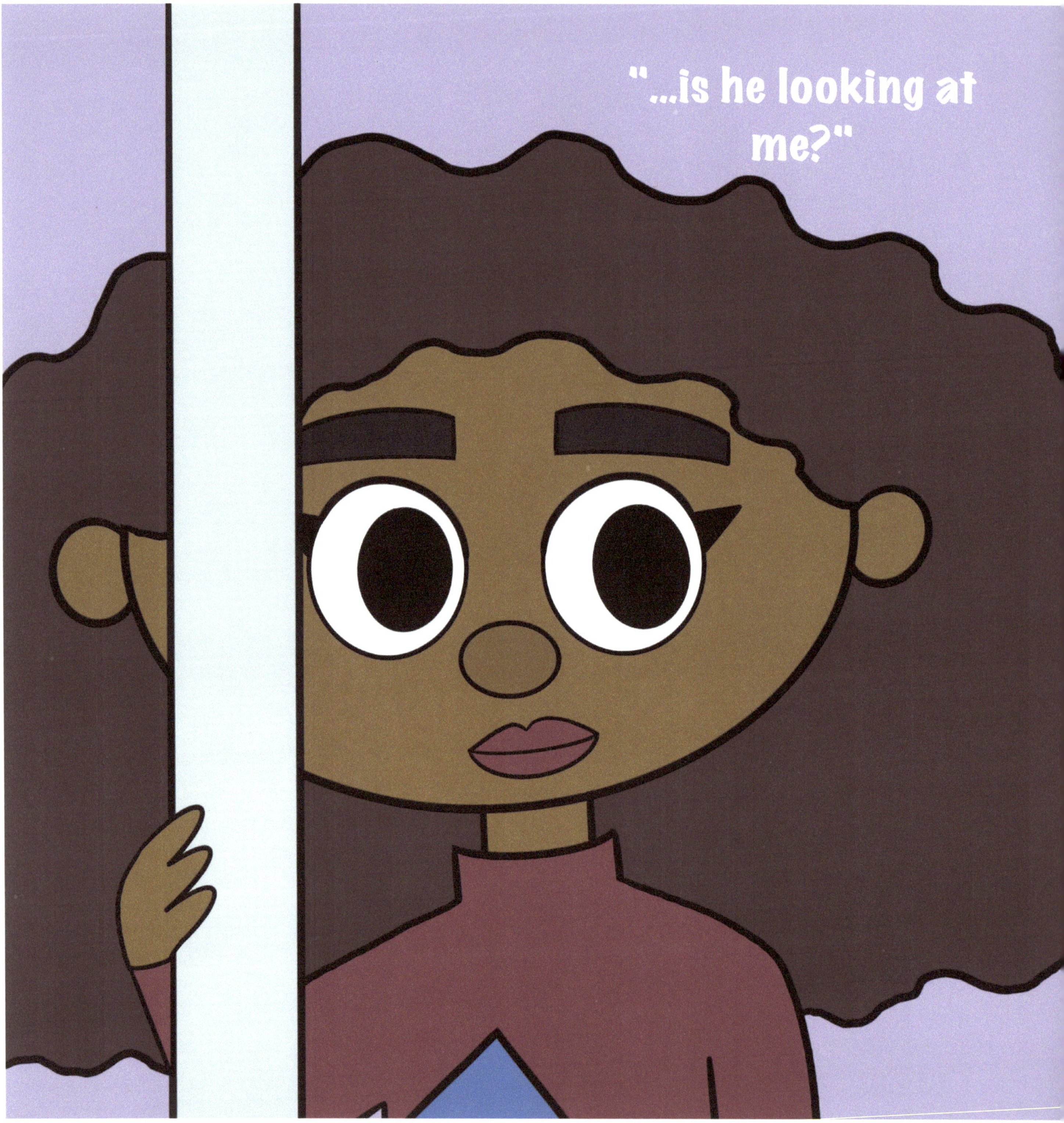
"...is he looking at me?"

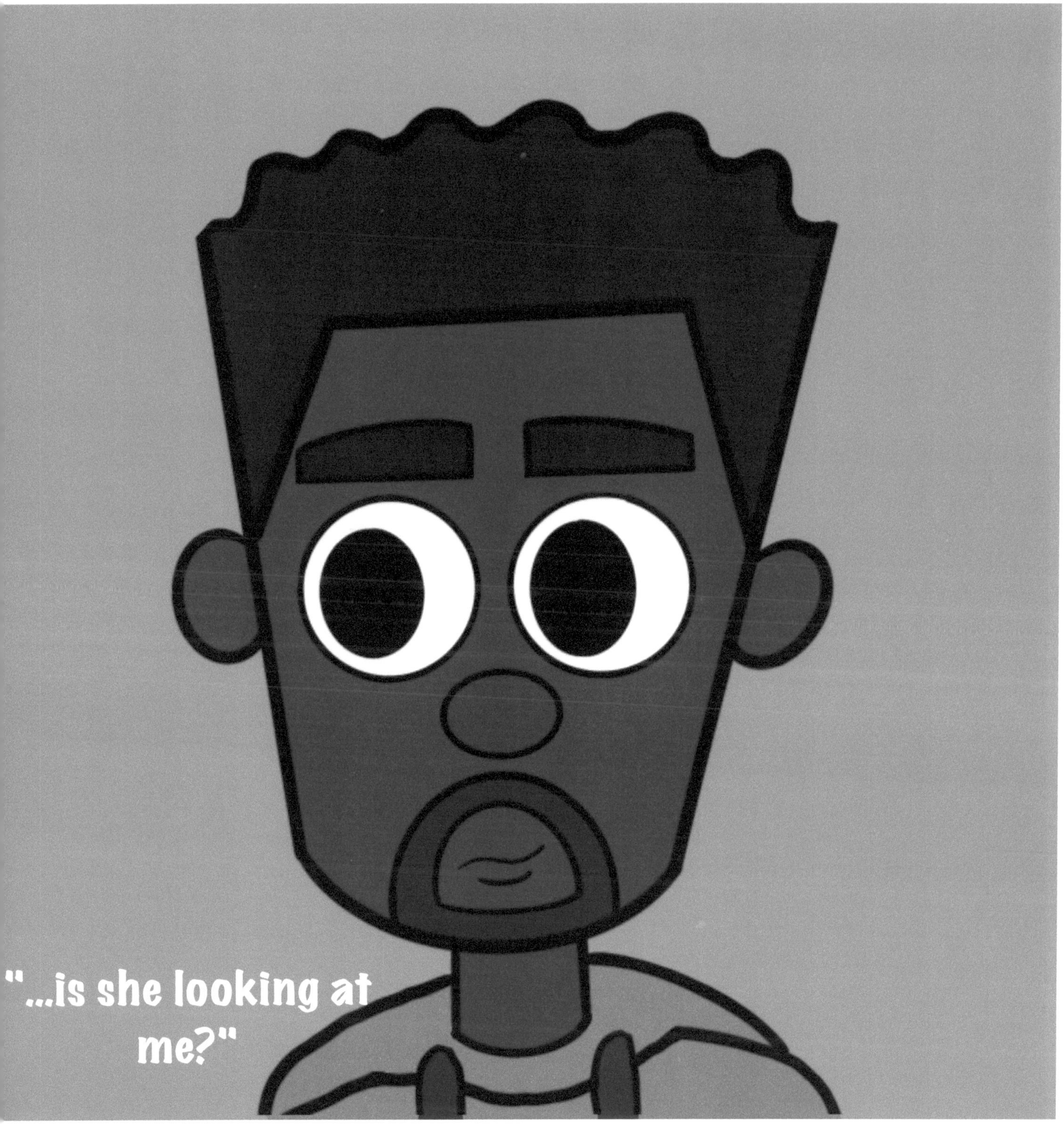
"...is she looking at me?"

Their eyes lock, time is taking a
freeze

"Is he actually looking at me?"

"Could she really be the one
from my dreams?"

Devon's heart stops beating,

is this real

or is his dream repeating...

Everything moves in slooww

motionnn.

It's almost like he's under water

or

under the spell of a love potion!

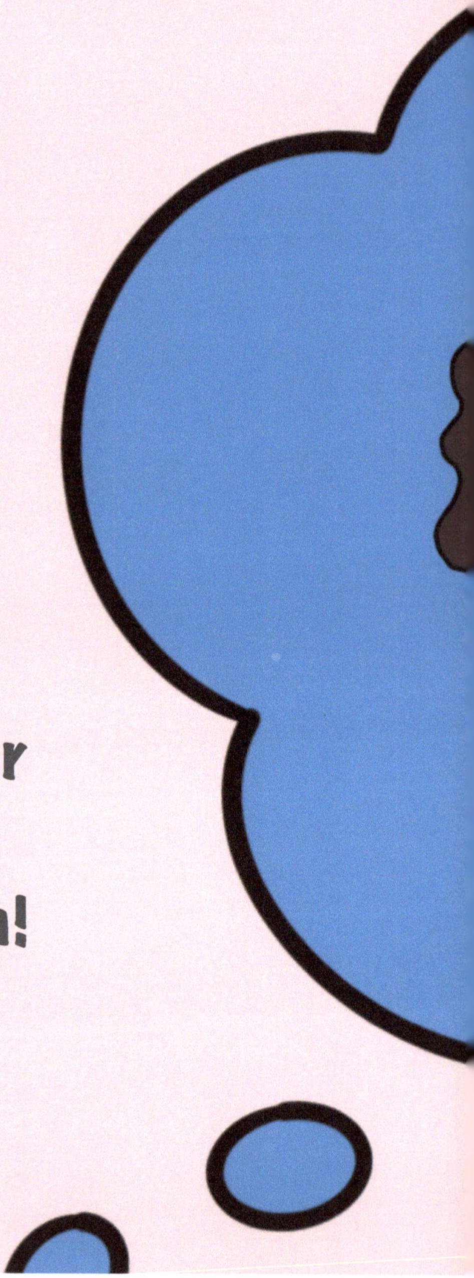

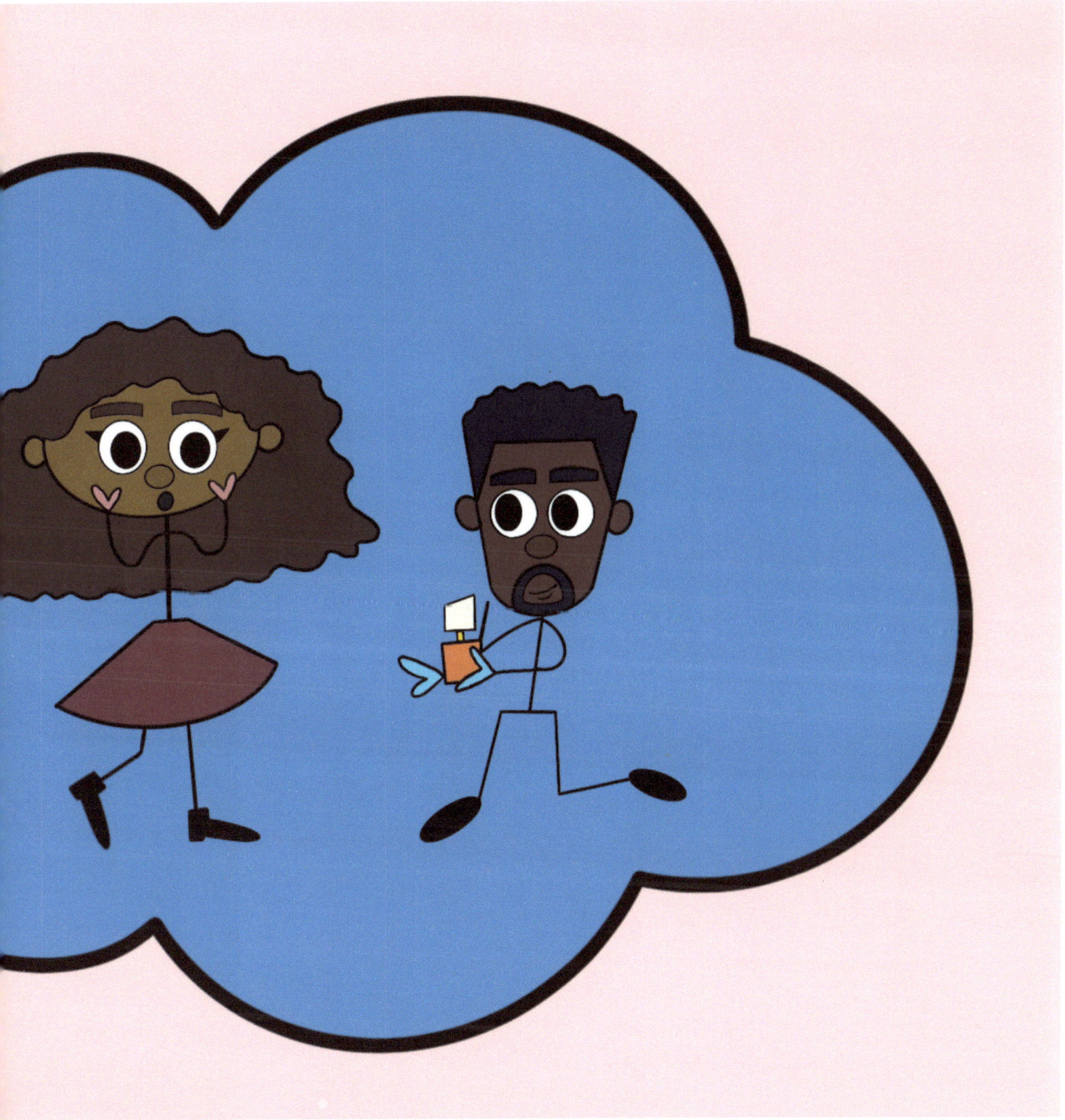

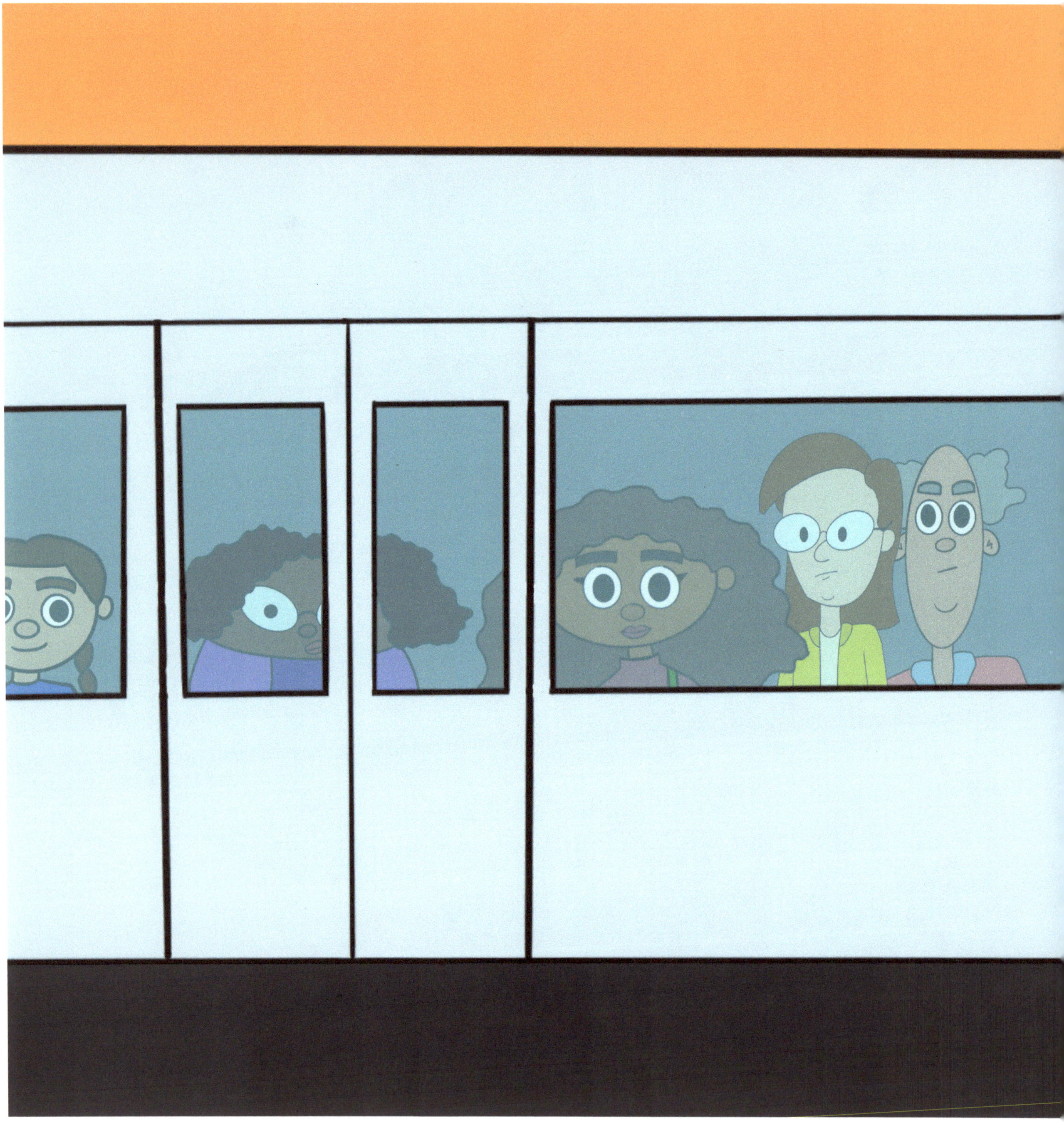

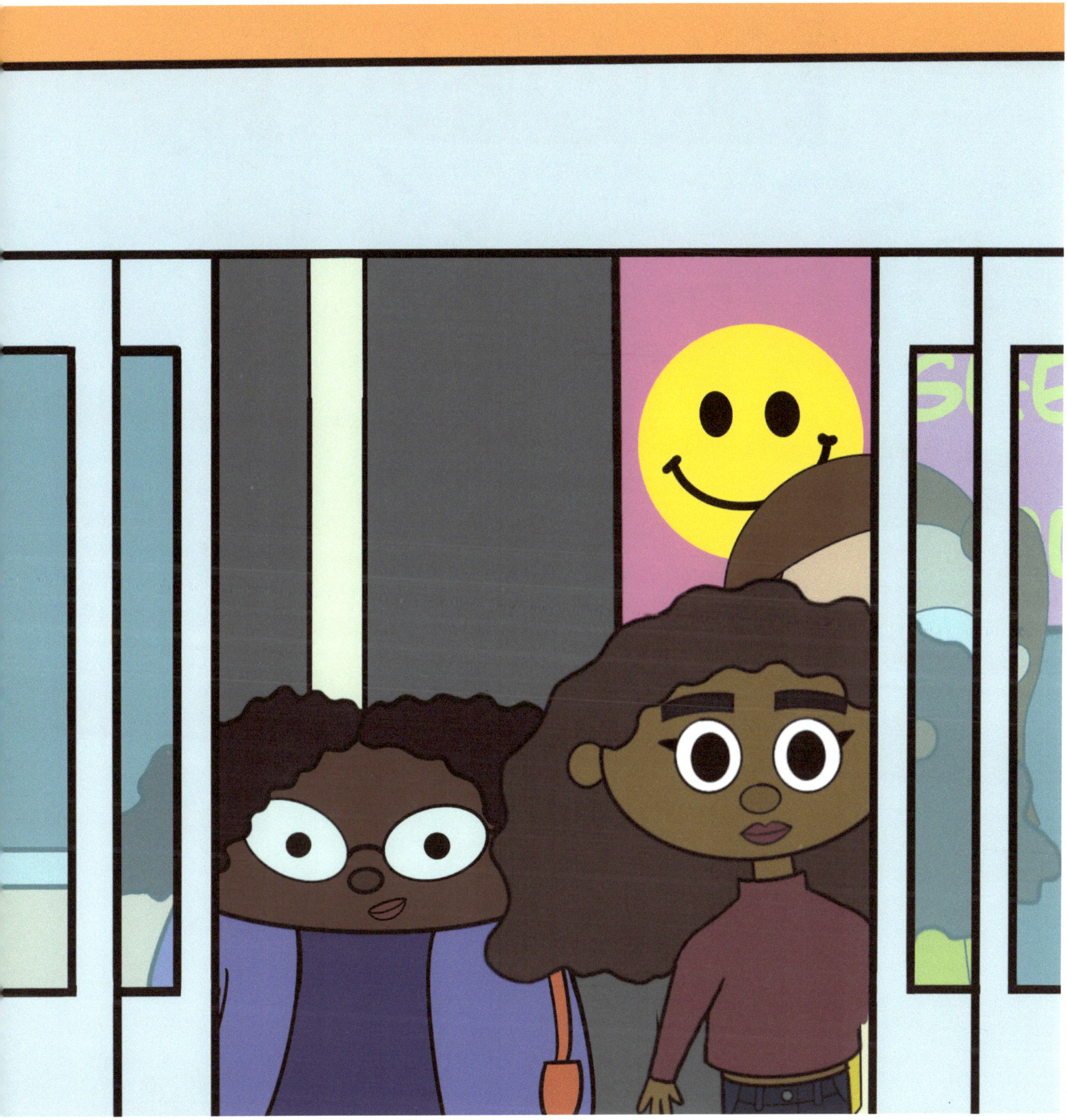

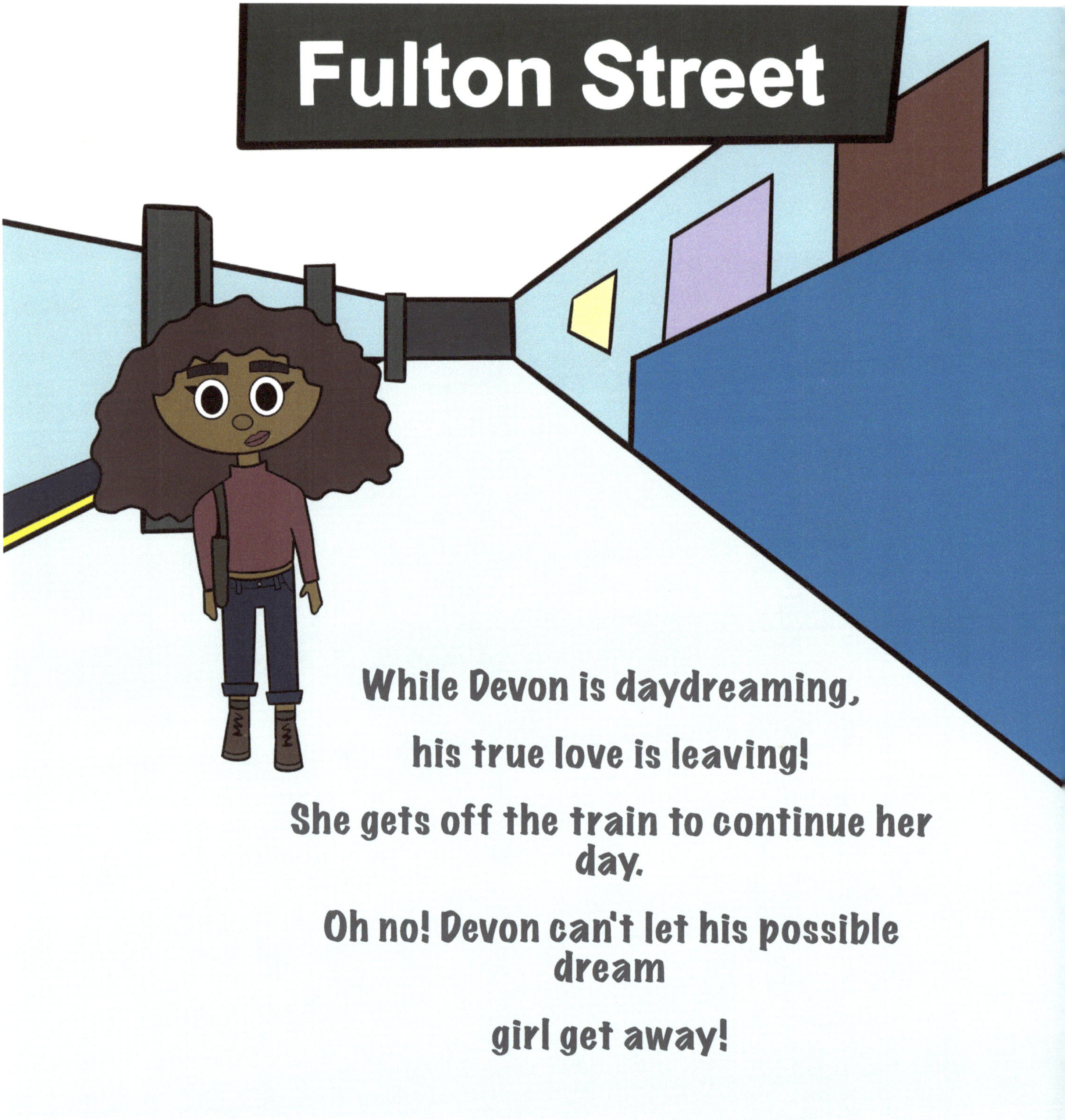
Fulton Street

While Devon is daydreaming,

his true love is leaving!

She gets off the train to continue her day.

Oh no! Devon can't let his possible dream

girl get away!

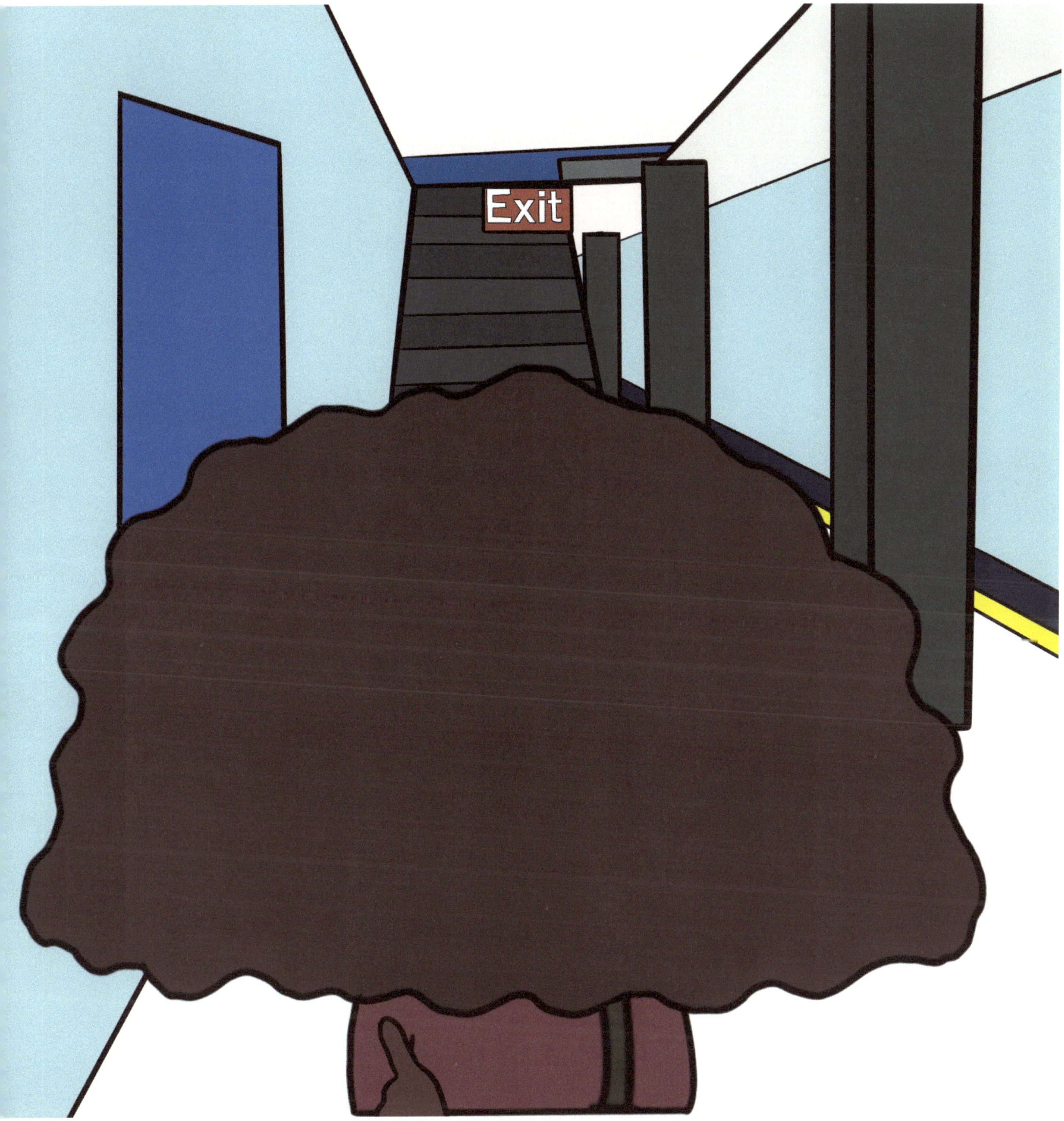
Exit

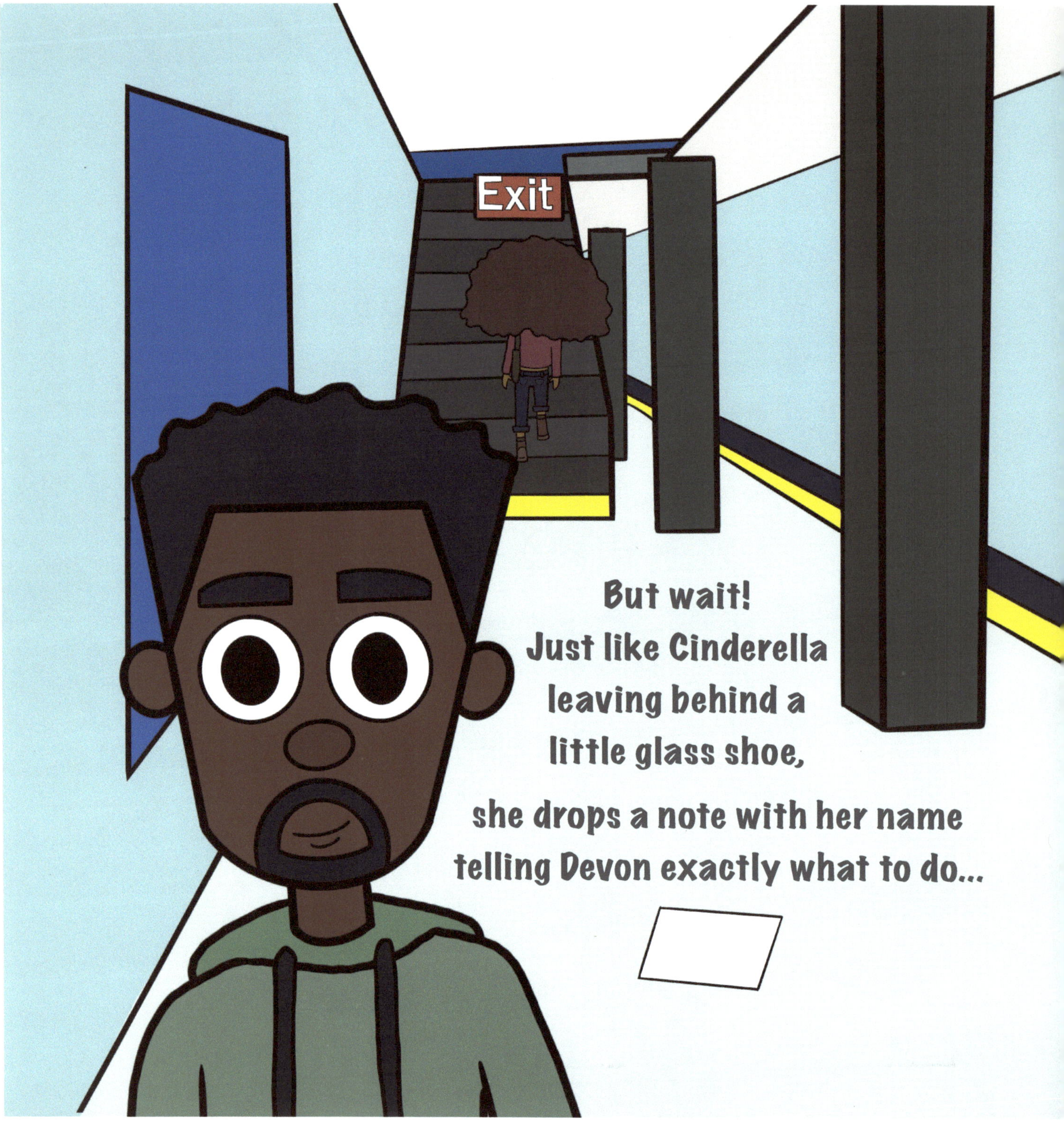
Exit
But wait!
Just like Cinderella
leaving behind a
little glass shoe,
she drops a note with her name
telling Devon exactly what to do...

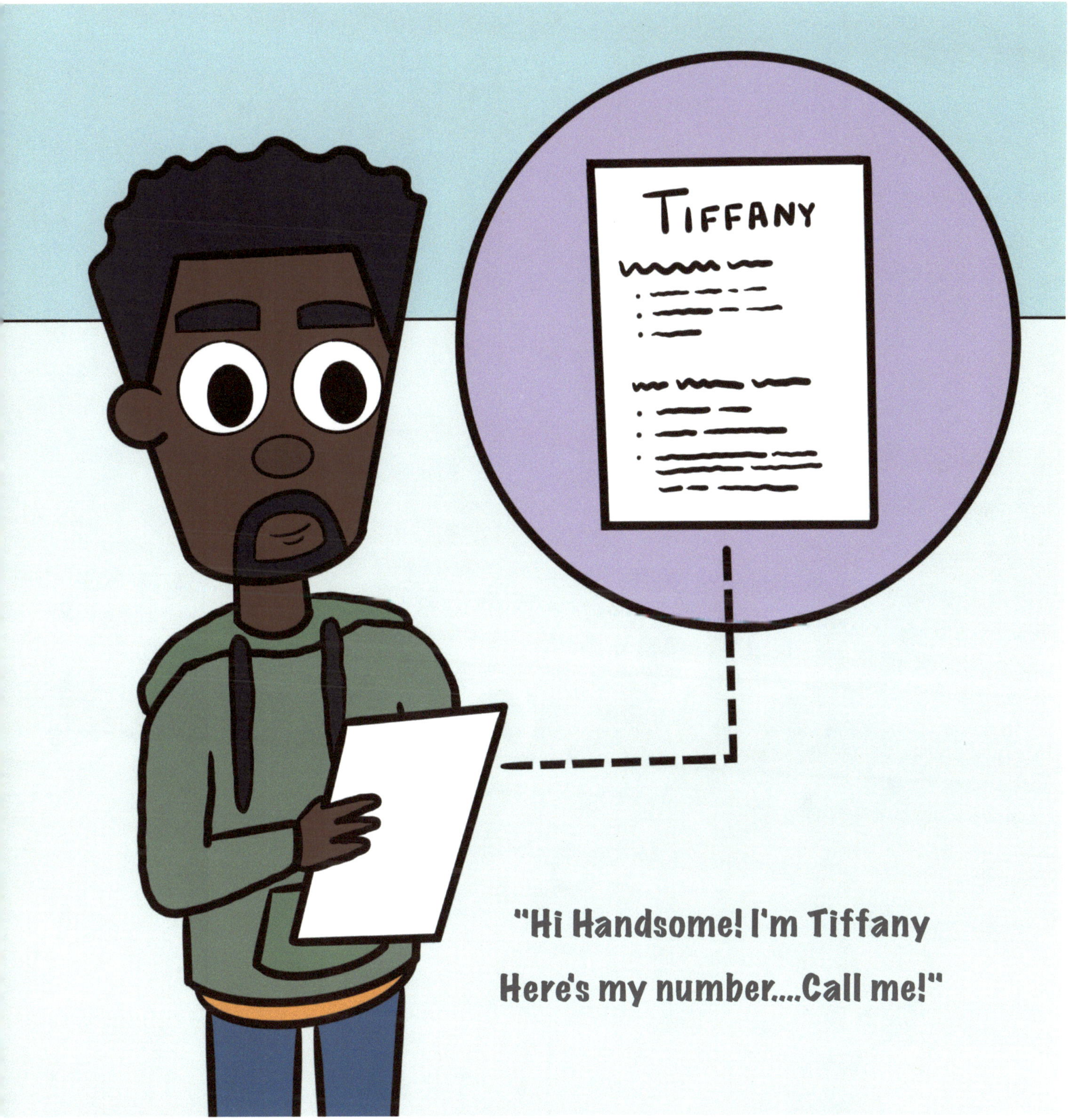
TIFFANY
"Hi Handsome! I'm Tiffany
Here's my number....Call me!"

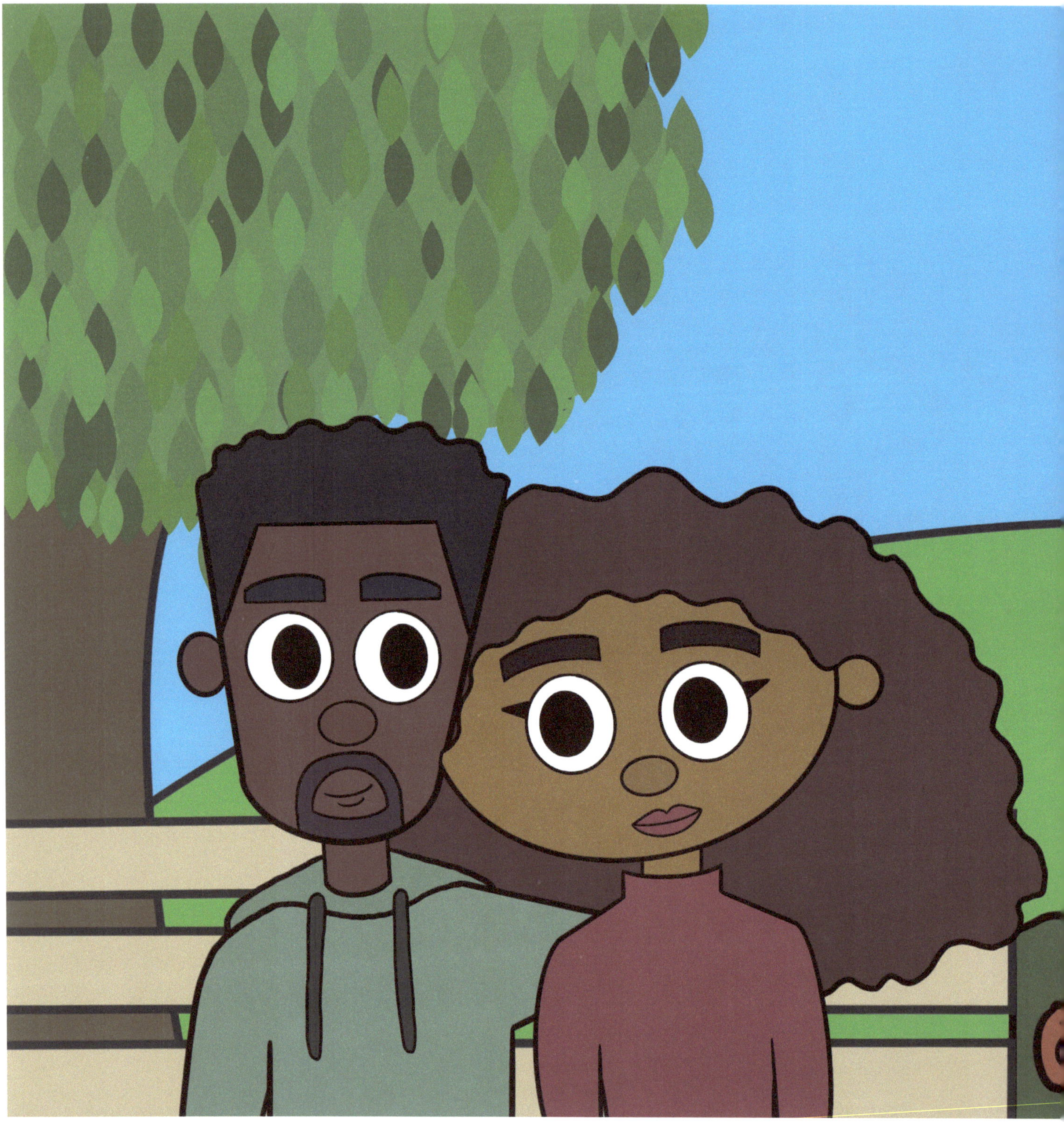

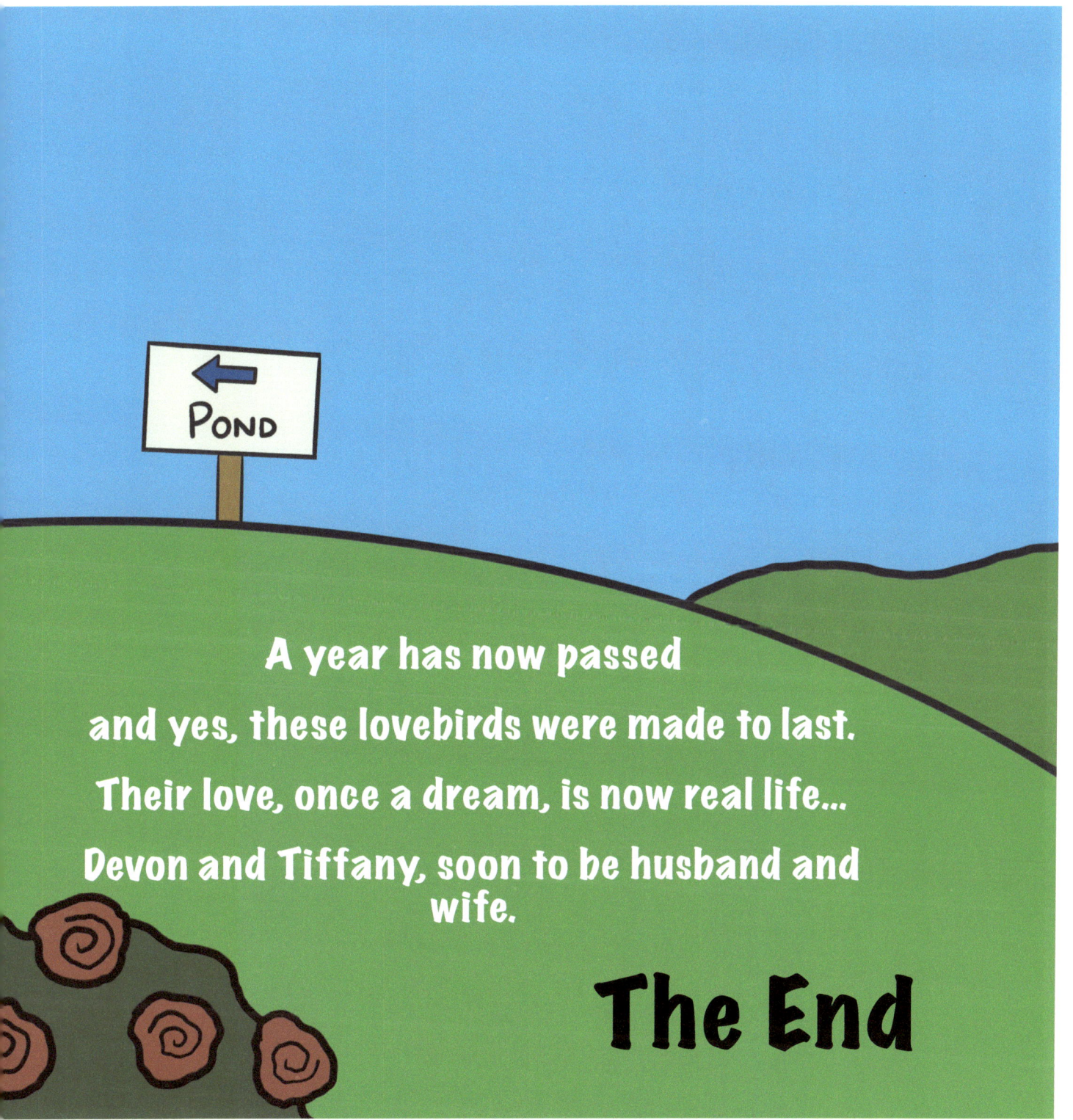

A year has now passed
and yes, these lovebirds were made to last.
Their love, once a dream, is now real life...
Devon and Tiffany, soon to be husband and wife.

The End

Interactive Lesson

Short Form and Multiple Choice Questions

1) Who is the protagonist in this story?

2) What does love mean to you?

48

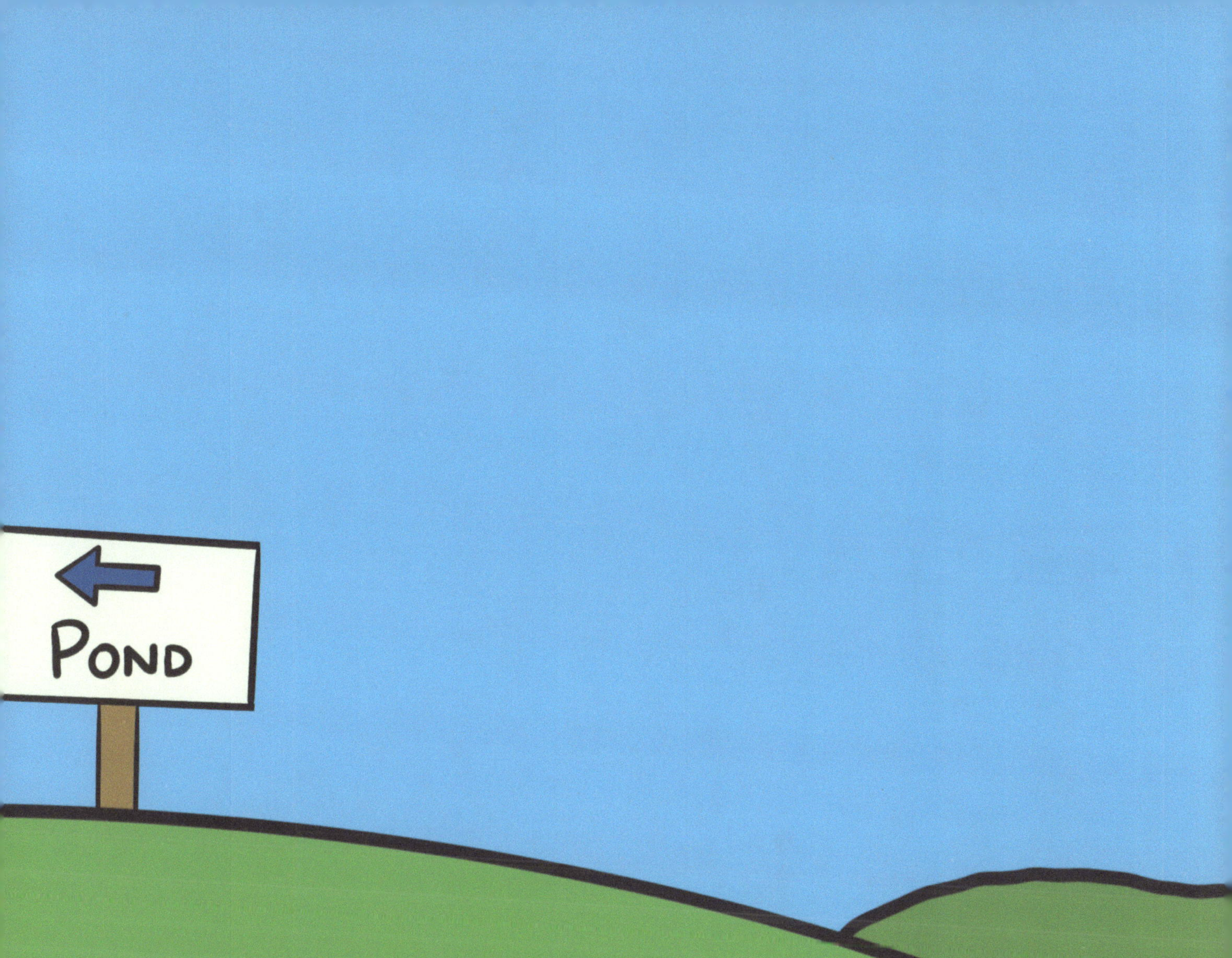
POND

3) What could have happened if Tiffany had not left the note on the ground?

a. Devon would never fall in love.

b. They would have met again someday.

c. Devon would have met someone else.

d. (Come up with your own ending)

4) Do you think Andrea's advice was helpful? Yes or no and why?

5) Have you ever had an experience where it felt like you were in a dream?

6) Has fear ever stopped you?

7) What's the best advice you've ever gotten?

8) "Is this the most beautiful girl or is Devon going insane...He pinches himself and tries to stay zen, could this just be Devon dreaming again?!"

What does "Zen" mean?

a. To get angry

b. To feel at peace and relaxed

c. To feel sick

9) How do you stay zen in your life?

10) Do you have a dream that you wish would come true?

Lesson Complete

Fill out your answers on a separate sheet of paper.

Thanks for your participation!

Draw and Color Section

Do you have a special wish or dream?

Draw a version of your own dream below:

Devon

Tiffany

Andrea

(Devon's Big Sister)

Website: www.truelovestorybook.com

To contact author: truelovestorybook@gmail.com

Follow Author on Instagram: @andreozim

Write a review: available on website

Printed in the USA
CPSIA information can be obtained
at www.ICGtesting.com
LVHW061158070224
771186LV00018B/448